Uberings

and

Uberchats

Following the Money

Emmanuel Nuvaga

Nuemman

An Imprint of Nuepress

Published by NuePress, a subsidiary of Nuemman LLC. NuePress books may be purchased in bulk for educational, business, or sales promotional use. For information please write:
NuePress, 10533 Cochron Dr., McKinney, TX 75070.
sales@nuepress.com

Designed by Emmanuel Nuvaga

Library of Congress Control Number: 2019905047

Emmanuel, Nuvaga (Emmanuel Nuvaga), 1976-
Uberings and Uberchats: Following the Money / Emmanuel Nuvaga. — 1st ed., May 2019
p. Cm.
Includes bibliographical references and index.
ISBN 978-1-7338163-1-1 (hardcover),
ISBN 978-1-7338163-3-5 (ebook)
ISBN 978-1-7338163-5-9 (paperback)
1. Neuropsychology. 2. Public Transportation. 3. Artificial Intelligence (AI). 4. Personal Success. I. Title

This book is dedicated to my late sister Judith Loga Caspa.

I love you Ma Lo....

CONTENTS

PREFACE

I wrote <u>Uberings and Uberchats: Following the Money</u> to literally follow the money and educate you, the intelligent and thoughtful reader, about the ride-sharing industry from an insider's perspective. Utilizing my technology and research background, I analyze Uber's use of artificial intelligence (AI) and other technologies that power and helped grow the company from a disruptive, innovative startup into a transportation giant. I lead you through my frustrations as Uber manipulates me and takes control of my life, making me more dependent on its platform as I help the company compensate for its massive driver attrition rate.

I want to help you translate information running in the background of your smartphone into your personal life so that you understand AI as it is utilized by major companies like Uber, Amazon, Facebook, Google, and Lyft. My psychological analysis of various events that occur between me and the Uber app, as well as some rider and other interactions, is intended as a roadmap for your enlightenment. As a driver, I try to engage you in a ride with me as I navigate my vehicle under the influence of my phone (DUIMP) which is just an ornament with a user interface under the influence of AI. My phone is controlled during ride-sharing by apps that micro-target me and, for the most part, take over my life until that point at which I am able to temporarily regain control.

By using establishing psychological principles and offering my insights gained from experience (or at least posing questions, given how little we know about many of these fast-growing companies that thrive from collecting, manipulating and selling information about us) I aim to help you understand the impact of new and imposing technologies like AI, machine learning and deep mining. I want you to see how these technologies are all being used by contemporary companies like Uber, Lyft, Amazon, Google and Facebook, among others, to control almost every aspect of our lives.

I didn't write this book bring negative attention to any of the companies I mention. My goal is to help you understand how they operate and make sense of your transactions with them. They're obviously here to stay and will be a significant part of our lives either directly or indirectly going forward, whether you use them or try to ignore them. I address some of their weaknesses or limitations, legal or inherent per their business models and categories, and make a business case for some of their current technologies, utilities or any future potential opportunities as I perceive them.

Despite the shroud of secrecy that surrounds these AI-operated and data-driven firms, I try to make the most of the limited information available to the public and give you the opportunity to understand and possibly infer their various potentials. Much of the research available to the public involved indirect access to consumer and driver data accounts linked to TNCs. Such indirect sources include emails (invoice), bank/credit card accounts (rider trip payments and driver salaries), app downloads tracking, driver and passenger surveys, and interviews and publications by Uber executives and insiders.

Rather than offering a top-down inference or analysis on driver-level behaviors and earnings by Uber and its associates, I draw from personal accounts as an Uber driver and from my research, clinical, technological and life experiences to analyze and give a bottom-up driver experience to the whole behavioral aspects that Uber brings to economics and psychology

I want this book to be a foundational guide and a constant read if and when you enter into a transaction with any of these companies, read or hear about them in the news, feel their transformational effects in your community, or become frustrated by their targeted advertising or invasion of and/or use of your privacy without your knowledge or consent.

Let's follow the money!

Emmanuel Nuvaga

nuvaga_business@hotmail.com

Dallas, Texas May 8, 2019

Uberings

and

Uberchats

CHAPTER 1

INTRODUCTION

Think of <u>Uberings and Uberchats</u> as a platform for ongoing conversations about how people, goods and services move from one point to another and the ensuing interactions, conversations and cultural exchanges involved, as well as the underlying processes inherent in the fulfillment of these transactions. They include multiple players, from the consumer on the demand side to the driver on the supply side and a bunch of intermediaries that include transportation network companies (TNCs) like Uber and Lyft, and other service providers.

While these services have historically been provided by taxis in differing forms across different cities and cultures, the advent of modern technologies like AI dramatically transforms human mobility and that of goods and services with more efficient processes. These are made possible by integrated technologies condensed into smartphones for a cheap, convenient and hassle-free experience for the modern-day consumer.

Throughout the ages, from the use of humans and litters to camelbacks, horsebacks and chariots, canoes, ships and boats, locomotives, automobiles and airplanes that make up the modern-day taxis, mankind has continuously sought faster and more efficient means of transport from one point to another. Many of these transportation solutions played significant roles in human civilization and cultural integration. Whether used in the construction of great architecture such as the pyramids of Egypt, the destruction of civilization as seen during the First and Second World Wars, or in the exploration of the universe, human mobility and that of all associated goods and services continue to evolve. Today, they are dominated by railways, airplanes and road vehicles.

Fig. 1: European women carried on litter by Africans in Ouidah, Bas-Dahomey (Benin Republic). c.a. 1920s, Societe de Geographie (from The New York Public Library, NYPL).

The last decade has seen radical transformation of the age-old taxi industry which, since the introduction of automobiles, has steadily devolved in terms of the services it provides. This downhill spiral presented a golden opportunity for ambitious and creative entrepreneurs like Travis Kalanick and Garrett Camp, who founded Uber, and Lyft founders Logan Green and John Zimmer.

Merriam-Webster dictionary defines the prefix "über-" as "being a superlative example of its kind or class," while I have always assumed Lyft to be a twist on the word "lift." Combining both meanings, you will see how and why Uber and Lyft have transformed the taxi business.

Uber and Lyft are part of a group of disruptors (including Airbnb, Turo, Amazon Flex and others) that are remaking major sectors of the economy into a gig economy which mostly exploits human labor through independent work or contracts. About 8.4% of workers in the U.S. work primarily as independent contractors, up 22% since revolutionary players Uber and Lyft entered the gig economy. There are four types of workers in the gig economy: free agents (choose to, primary source of income), reluctants (prefer traditional jobs if available), casual earners (choose to, supplemental income), and financially strapped (have traditional jobs but need the money). Nonemployed individuals participate more (1.7%) than employed individuals (1.2%) in the transportation gig or "Uber" economy. Some 30% of the U.S. labor force or close to an estimated 60 million

Americans participate in independent work as a primary or secondary activity.

Ride-hailing companies may otherwise be referred to as ride-sharing, ride-sourcing, mobility services, car sharing or drive-sourcing companies, depending on their business model or activities. Founded in 2000, ZipCar was the first ride-hailing company, followed by Zimride in 2007 (which eventually became Lyft in 2013). UberCab launched in 2009 and Uber dominates the industry today with about 70% of U.S. ride-share spending in 2018.

Though Lyft was the pioneer in this transformation, Uber grew rapidly by mastering and deploying the integrated technologies that helped transform the ride-sharing industry. A number of competing companies have sprung up across the globe to seize control over local niches, and the transformation in mobility has further morphed into renting dock- less e-bikes and e-scooters.

Especially in the United States, with generational dependence and increasing adherence to personal and private car usage, a well-structured and conveniently-operated transportation service with value-added features that are consumer friendly and cost saving has a major role to play in the future of mobility. These services depend on the endpoint customer-facing drivers, who are the main point of contact as operators of the vehicles that transport people, goods and services from one point to another.

Fig 2: Uber takes advantage and stretches its technology to destroy the taxi business.

It should be noted that an impending transition designed to phase out any need for human drivers is coming...sooner than you might think. The future of mobility points more towards driverless cars, many of which are currently being tested by several companies. These vehicles will undoubtedly decrease cost and increase efficiency with regard to vehicle usage and road safety. At the same time, they threaten to worsen already decreasing human societal interactions which driver-dependent ride-sharing encourages by connecting people who probably have never met and may never meet again.

Beyond the lean technologies ride-sharing companies have leveraged to dramatically improve the transportation industry where taxis especially were failing, Uber and Lyft continue to burn through cash at a breathtaking rate. These financial shortcomings stem from the fact that the majority of services provided by predominantly passenger transporting companies involve human beings. The value of their lives is immeasurable and their behaviors are often unpredictable, sometimes involving inherent risks. Ride- sharing companies are certainly aware of these limitations and are, consequently, diligently working to limit or eliminate human-dependent risk factors, as evidenced in their pursuit of driverless cars and technologies.

Driverless vehicles are still several decades from dominating public transportation, so TNCs like Uber and Lyft depend on humans to execute the endpoint operation of transporting people, goods and services from one point to another. The result is that many decisions the TNCs have made both in their corporate structures and in their partnerships with many drivers have ramifications that extend beyond their investors to encompass society as a whole.

In an effort to lure customers away from the increasingly expensive and poorly-operated taxi industry, many TNCs combine attractively low fares with improved services. This is possible because many of the TNCs do not own or operate fleets of vehicles; therefore, they don't bear a lot of the operation and maintenance costs of running a car. That falls to the drivers, who spread associated risk and liabilities across their communities.

Uber and Lyft have experienced exponential and explosive growth in their decade of existence, despite being unprofitable with billions of dollars in annual losses. Such growth presents greater opportunities to expand their markets, currently dominated by large cities and metropolitan areas, into smaller cities and suburbs. Recent service offerings include bike and scooter rentals, as well as food and package deliveries. Amazon is now viewed as a major player in the latter two categories.

Despite these opportunities and a fast-growing market, TNCs continue to bleed losses from operational costs and insurance liabilities per ridership. Significant losses also stem from discounts offered to customers and bonuses or commissions offered to their partner drivers. Within the context of this book, I explain operational costs, losses and value projects from the driver perspective. I "follow the money" to earn income, but additionally have direct exposure to the thousands of invoices generated automatically after each ride.

For example, a major trip cost component that helps TNCs keep overall fares low for their customers is the use of dynamic or "surge" pricing. As these companies go public where they will face greater scrutiny, they've restructured the surge pricing algorithms to add a proprietary control and covert determination of trip fares that go beyond the AI psychological manipulation of both drivers and riders when demand is high and supply is low.

Uber surge pricing has transitioned from geometric multipliers like 1.0x, 1.6x 2.0x, and 2.1 x of the original trip fare to arithmetic additions of dollar amounts like $1.0, $2.72, and $5.8 to the original trip fare. The result is that drivers are no longer able to calculate a trip cost or evaluate their earnings potential. The arithmetic surge pricing system has a geometric unexplained component where an advertised trip of $9.00 may actually pay the driver the surge multiplier, something I have experienced with long- distance trips.

Companies like Uber rely heavily on psychological manipulations of human impulses and compulsion to expand and maintain both their ridership and pool of drivers. Given the flexibility and convenience drivers are offered—with no contract obligations on wages and benefits—it isn't difficult to manipulate drivers whose impulses tend to push them toward making more money with less effort when a customer pays a higher price for the same ride.

As a driver, I literally follow the surge heat maps in an attempt to get rides that pay higher fares. Surge pricing also takes advantage of customers' compulsion when faced with a situation where they might fear the risk of not being able to have a ride home after big events like football games, inclement weather, alcohol consumption, or any environment where there is a low supply of drivers.

Technology startups like Uber are radically addressing and transforming age-old areas of our lives that have been run inefficiently for generations. Innovative entrepreneurs and risk-takers, inspired after experiencing challenges in using some of these services, devoted their time, effort and resources to design simplistic and more efficient solutions which leverage modern technologies.

AI and other technologies are still in their early phases of development, but have the potential to significantly transform human civilization as we further develop and exploit their potentials in the coming years. This requires resources to both train and hire expert engineers, as well as develop the complex computers and network equipment, and other necessary applications. Innovation is expensive, so relatively new companies like Uber are often financed through venture capitalists who offer the initial seed money in the early phases of the development.

Both Uber and Lyft have burned through colossal sums of money. But just look at the products and services that have resulted from venture-backed research and development and how efficiently they have transformed various sectors of Uber and Lyft's business categories. It takes a lot of resources to accomplish such transformations and a lot of money to finance those resources.

Amazon is another which is already making significant moves into the logistics sector while quietly expanding its network of driver partners and airline fleet.

No one truly knows the real cost of an average Uber or Lyft ride. Their reported standards vary by different localities and any applied subsidies, and prices may be dramatically escalated depending on whether they were surging. A change in the advertised route can increase the trip advertised cost by multiple folds and while Uber automatically makes an adjustment to the surge, it doesn't explain what algorithm it uses. The company reports that "in certain markets, its pricing technology decouples consumer and driver pricing, such that the consumer pays an upfront price, which is calculated based on the estimated trip time and distance from origin to destination as well as demand patterns for that route at that time, while the driver earns an amount that is based off their time and distance traveled." Decoupling the rider from the driver essentially leaves Uber in control and without an upfront conversation between the two car-coupled strangers, the driver only finds out his/her payment at the end of the trip, although the rider may have been given a quote before booking the trip.

Uber and Lyft advertise upfront pricing that shows customers the price they will pay at the end of the ride before it begins. That price might vary based on changes in the route that may increase or decrease the trip distance, trip duration and any applicable tolls.

Knowing the true value of a ride is paramount to determining and valuating companies like Uber and Lyft. Future price hikes are imminent and imperative to ensure their paths to profitability, which will only come when they start eliminating a lot of the subsidies they have offered their ridership over the past decade. Uber riders currently only pay about 40% of the true cost of their rides.

Although TNCs depend and operate on novel technologies, they still observe standard practices in the transportation business, such as maintaining general liability insurance on their customers and drivers. Many Americans, especially those in the older generation, are afraid to get into a private car as a means of public transportation. They're not just being irrationally fearful; there is supporting evidence of passengers being assaulted by their drivers, and several cases in which drivers have been assaulted by unruly passengers.

Uber has also faced complaints of a "culture of sex" in its corporate structure during the reign of its founding CEO, Travis Kalanick. Lyft's recent IPO (initial public offering) filing showed that just over 50% of its total cost of revenues is insurance-related. These companies still require all participating drivers to carry basic liability insurance on any car used in ride-sharing, but some major insurance companies in the country do not underwrite policies for drivers involved in ride-sharing.

Uber is here to stay, and the $36 billion ride-hailing ("Uber") economy is still just a small part of a nearly $6 trillion worldwide transportation services market. TNCs have plenty of room to grow as long as they continue to provide better pricing and services, and innovate in an industry where taxis have failed for years despite a global taxi market worth $108 billion. Globally, authorities are increasingly choosing to adopt Transportation Network Company (TNC) regulations.

With Lyft and Uber going public with IPOs this year, we should all continue to ask questions regarding their financial statements, the true cost of a ride, their surge algorithms, and their true market value. Given that these startups have grown into mammoth corporations, with many of their practices remaining covert, this book is just a first step in answering some of those questions. I wrote it from driver's perspective in an attempt to shed light on the operations of companies like Uber and Lyft and the impact they have on the various stakeholders involved, especially drivers.

We are the backbone of their current business models, so we have a huge stake in their future strategic objective of using driverless cars.

CHAPTER 2

STAKEHOLDERS

The sprawling sharing economy helps meet the demand for pooled goods and services by using individuals eager to make money from the products they own or services they can provide, as well as companies that broker the transactions or supply assets. This means a lot of stakeholders and partnerships are involved in making your Uber ride as seamless and fulfilling as possible, and for most people it has been an overwhelmingly positive experience that has addressed gaps and failures from their previous taxi experiences.

A lot of the partnerships have been contracted by the TNC that is providing the intermediation service and the customer or the driver maybe surprised to know that many similar transactions they effect in their other daily life activities are also involved in facilitating their ride-sharing experience. But there are also several other stakeholders that are visibly involved, some directly in helping fulfill the transactions, while others may just be casualties from the innovation and transformation brought by TNCs.

This means that there are several relationships of different characters involved: employment, taxation, public policy, economic justice, human health, and behavioral issues are just a few.

The Uber economy sprang from the taxi industry and involves the following stakeholders:

1. Transportation Network Companies (TNCs)

TNCs, also known as ride-hailing companies, use digital technology platforms to provide rides by connecting passengers with drivers, thereby giving consumers more transportation options. Users can request rides through a smartphone app or website that connects riders with nearby drivers. Payments are typically handled through a credit card linked to the app and riders are charged a trip fee comprised of service, booking, a base fare, cost per minute and cost per mile, all of which may vary between cities. The biggest ride-sharing companies by market valuation are Uber, Lyft, Curb (used by cabs), Didi Chuxing, Grab, Ola, Careem (Middle East), Taxify. Uber is by far the largest of these companies, while Didi is the major player in China, Ola Cabs is the largest transportation company in India and Grab is Southeast Asia's biggest ride-hailing app.

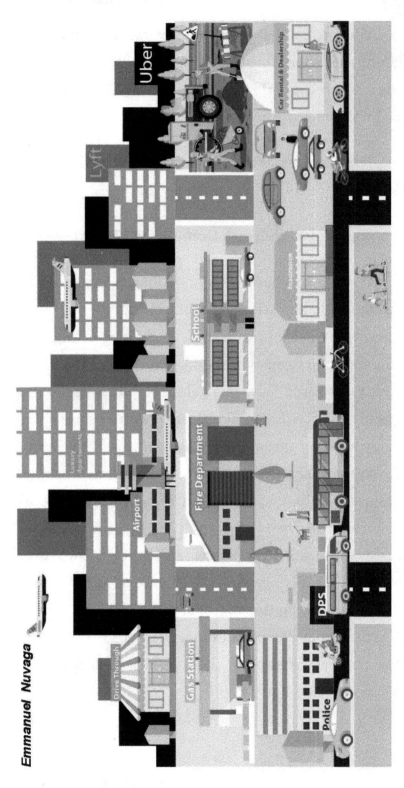

Emmanuel Nuvaga

Fig. 3: Major stakeholders in the ride-sharing economy.

Newer companies Lime, Bird and Skip have taken this concept into bike sharing and scooter sharing in downtowns areas of some major U.S. cities. Lyft acquired the bike- rental service Motivate, Ford acquired dockless bike and e-scooter startup Spin, and Uber acquired JUMP Bikes, a clear indication of this spaces potential. Uber also bought Middle-East rival Careem for $3.1 billion early this year and is investing heavily in freight shipments.

About 70% of the U.S. market is dominated by Uber compared to about 29% for Lyft. Gett (Juno) and Via are smaller players. Via is contracted with the City of Arlington, TX for most of its public transportation needs, given that it is the largest city in the United States (population 396,407) without mass transit. The Dallas-Fort Worth Metroplex has a new ride-share startup, Alto. A tracking of the monthly ride-share market growth by the analytics company Second Measure shows similar growth trends and patterns, and although Lyft is growing faster, any news or changes in the market affect both companies.

2. Transporting Vehicle and Ride Options

Transportation companies have varying requirements and different vehicle options. They may include a cut-off age, number of doors and minimum number of seat belts for the vehicle, as well as current registration, insurance, and compliance with local statutes.

Uber and Lyft maintain automobile liability insurance on behalf of all U.S. partners and various vehicle options. Uber has UberX, UberXL, Black, Black SUV, UberBlack and UberSelect, which require commercial insurance and ratings requirements based on the market. In 2017, Uber launched UberMoto (motorized bikes in India), UberGo (chauffeur-driven hatchbacks in India), UberSelect (my favorite, but strangely not featured in Uber's IPO filing), UberVip (exclusively offered to American Express Consumer Platinum® and Centurion® Cardholders), Uber Bus, UberAuto (India) and Uber HIRE (India). Lyft offers its standard service Lyft, plus Lyft Lux, Lux Black, and Lux Black XL.

These various Uber and Lyft vehicle options range from sedan, minivans, SUVs, wheelchair accessible vehicles, luxury cars and limousines. Shared trips, which pickup additional passenger(s) after the first passenger(s) boards are Uber POOL and Lyft Line, while in Uber Express POOL and Lyft Shared Rides, passengers walk to a pickup location to accommodate stops and turns, and any driving inconveniences. Uber Bus matches up to 14 riders in one large minibus. All rides in this book refer to the basic standard ride options of UberX and Lyft, unless otherwise specified.

3. Drivers

Today's ride-hailing drivers assume the job historically performed by taxi drivers and in contemporary American metropolitan cities, taxi drivers have mostly been immigrants. Historical statistics from New York City shows the percentage of the city's immigrant taxi and livery drivers was 38% in 1980, 64% in 1990, and 84% in 2000. The racial, ethnic, native language as well as educational attainment levels for taxi and livery drivers in New York City show that Haitians dominated in the 80s with French as native language, Asians, especially Pakistanis, dominated in the 90s, speaking native Pakistani and Urdu; while the dominant drivers today are Bengali-speaking Bangladeshis, Spanish-speaking Dominicans and Pakistanis.

In New York City today, Bangladeshis make up the majority of taxi drivers, while Dominicans dominate for-hire vehicle drivers. The majority of these individuals had attended or graduated from college and in 2016, about 25% of taxi drivers and chauffeurs nationwide majored in business. The percentage of newly-licensed drivers from Egypt, Morocco, Ghana and Nigeria rose from 9.2% in 1991 to 14.5% in 2000, reflecting the growing population of Africans in New York City. In the DFW area, I see increasing numbers of African immigrants in the ride-sharing economy, with many Northeast Africans driving UberBlack, limos and taxis.

According to the 2000 census, 38% of taxi and limousine drivers nationwide were immigrants, bypassed only by tailors and farm laborers in occupations with at least 50,000 workers. In 2016, 51.9% of taxi drivers and chauffeurs nationwide were white, 25.9% were black or African American, 11.7% were Asian and 14% were women. Also in 2016, the median age of taxi drivers and chauffeurs was 46.7, and male employees were generally 1.91 years older than their female counterparts. There are more male drivers, 76%, than female drivers on the Uber platform.

In early 2018, Uber's Chief Economist Jonathan Hall reported that more than 750,000 people drive with Uber in the United States but Uber's IPO filing reports 3.9 million drivers worldwide without distinguishing how many are in the US. In a Stanford study in partnership with Uber that involved Mr. Hall, they reported 1.9 million people drove for Uber between January 2015 and March 2017. Lyft's IPO filing reports 1.4 million drivers (US and Canada), 34% of whom are over the age of 45 and 9% are veterans of the armed forces. Uber reported more than 200,000 drivers in Egypt and more than 100,000 drivers in Saudi Arabia.

It is therefore reasonable to assume that more than 3 million Americans work for these two companies. Given the fact that a significant chunk of their revenue and operations are based in the United States, it is also plausible to assume that Uber and Lyft were important stakeholders employing at least 2% of the 156 million Americans who were employed in the labor force in 2018 and this trend is likely to continue.

These historical trends and recent statistics support the fact that virtually all kinds of people work in the taxi and ride-sharing economy. In my ride-sharing driving experience I have met a pilot, flight attendant, doctors, pharmacists, tenured economist, MBA holders, veterans, retirees, students, middle-aged men and women and plenty of young adults who all drive for transportation network companies. Some drive full-time and others part-time as an added source of income. Many retirees find it to be a beneficial way to stay active while earning money and enjoying conversations (or uberchats) with a broad range of people. These different stakeholders may have variant prospects, expectations, or utility valuations for their participation in ride- sharing.

4. Riders

Ride-hailers come from all walks of life and all classes and corners of society. As a driver, I meet professionals traveling to and from work, students headed to school, patients going to the hospital, fans attending sporting or social events, travelers headed to or from the airport, partying and club-hopping socialites, cheaters or partners leaving their boyfriend or girlfriend's house in the dark of night, and people just trying to get to the corner store to buy a cigarette or burger. You name it, I've driven them.

Millennials (the 18–34 demographic) appear to place less importance on car ownership than previous generations, and tend to take more Uber rides than any other age demographic. The average active Uber riders are in their mid-20s with an above-average income and, like 83% of urban dwellers, own smartphones. Older Uber riders take longer and more expensive rides, while more affluent riders take more rides and are more likely to use more expensive types of Uber services, such as UberBlack. An independent study found that the vast majority of Uber riders are Whites (80.5%), while Hispanics (8.5%), African-Americans (8.2%), and Asian-Americans (2.8%) take far fewer rides.

5. Roads

It takes a network of routes to move a person or freight from point A to point B. Ride- hailing exploits the sophisticated and vast network of roads mostly in urban

American metropolitan cities. The U.S. has about 4 million miles (6.44 million kilometers) of public roads, of which about 2.3 million miles or 1.43 million kilometers (59%) are paved. In 2008, roads in rural constituted 73.4% of this mileage but urban (areas with population of 5,000 or more) mileage constituted only 26.6% yet carried 60.1% of the 3.0 trillion VMT.

Roads are classified on the basis of the types of function provided: (1) inter- state highways, (2) arterials, (3) collectors, and (4) local streets or access roads.

Arterial	Principal (Major)	Interstate
		Freeway/Expressway
		Other Principal
	Minor	
Collector	Major	
	Minor	
Local	Local Streets	

Fig. 4: Functional Road Classification (Federal Highway Administration, FHWA)

The Federal Highway Administration (FHWA) estimates that the current system of paved roads in 2018 handled a volume of traffic on the order of $3.2 \times$ trillion (or 3.2×10^{12}) vehicle miles traveled (VMT), or about 8 billion (8.8×10^9) vehicle miles per day. In 2008, local roads in rural areas made up 50.2% of total mileage but carried only 4.4% of total VMT, while the portion of the Interstate System in urban areas made up only 0.4% of total mileage but carried 15.2% of total VMT.

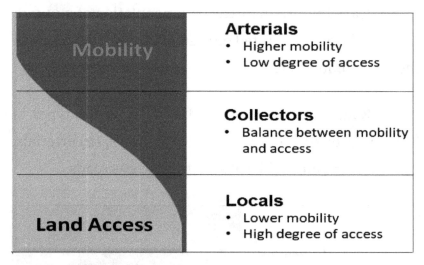

Fig. 5: Mobility and Road Access

About 0.75 billion miles (1.21 billion kilometers) per day for a total of 275 billion miles (442.57 billion kilometers) were driven in Texas in 2017. DFW Metroplex has an extensive network of broad and well-connected roads with worsening traffic flow despite the seemingly perpetual constructions and expansions seen at almost every corner of these networks.

6. Taxis

Taxis have been the primary means of transportation for generations and taxi driving has historically been the traditional route to upward mobility for entry level workers in the United States and other Western countries. This trend will likely continue in the new ride-sharing economy.

As businesses, taxi companies are required to have commercial taxi insurance, pay their workers a minimum wage and in some instances, provide health insurance and any other federal, state or city-mandated employment requirements to their workers based on the size of the business. In certain states and localities, chauffeur licensing exams and taxi driver training programs may require additional licenses that are often too expensive and hard to obtain, as is the case of Medallions in New York City. These factors put taxi companies at a disadvantage when faced with competition from technology-driven innovative ride-hailing companies.

7. Car Rentals

Rental car companies have historically been major players in ground transportation but ride sharing has changed that scenario. Today, it makes more sense for individuals to conveniently use ride-sharing for transportation if they are flying into another city instead of going through the hassle of picking up and dropping off an expensive rental car. Uber has even formed a partnership with Hertz, Fair and Getaround to facilitate drivers getting vehicles for ride-sharing. In 2015, Uber created Xchange Leasing to lease directly to drivers, but shut it down in 2018.

8. Insurance Companies

Insurance companies are important players in the ride-sharing economy given the inherent risks involved in hundreds of thousands of cars plying millions of miles daily and variant driver behaviors, especially in highly-congested cities. TNCs use third party insurance to insure the rider or passenger(s) and to cover partners and their vehicles when they are driving on the ride-sharing platform. Coverage that varies by state can be up to $1,000,000 ($1.25 million in New York City). Driver partners are required to have insurance that covers their vehicle when they are not driving on these platforms. Moreover, a basic general liability policy that meets these requirements is mandatory, although the insurance requirements may vary from a general liability to a commercial policy based on the service option.

9. Local Communities

The stakes of local communities in the ride-sharing economy are huge, given the range of services that transportation network companies provide. This involves changes in traffic patterns within the communities, businesses that may benefit or suffer from the presence of such companies, invasion of high-end estates that were probably built with exclusion or seclusion in mind, and changes in legislation to either accommodate or restrict TNCs. There is also increased spending in emergency services and personnel in response to the changes brought by the presence of TNCs, and the impact of TNC services on the communal behaviors of various members of these communities, from children to the elderly, and from drivers to riders.

Other stakeholders include commuters in their private cars, business vehicles, bike and scooter riders, pedestrians, city and airport management, local businesses, individual residences and estates, small and big businesses and partners that provide services to all the aforementioned stakeholders, as well as the broader public at large.

The USPS, UPS and FedEx have delivered packages for decades, but such previous transactions by volumes and number of deliverers is nowhere near the complex networks of package delivery services and companies servicing these exclusive communities today, from mail to food to e-commerce packages.

CHAPTER 3

INTEGRATED TECHNOLOGIES

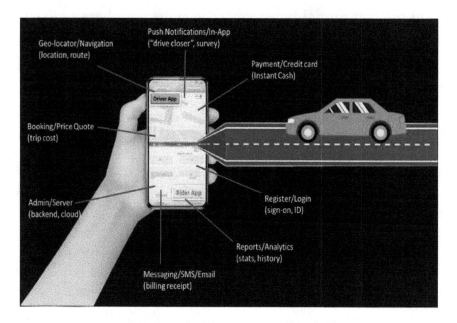

Fig. 6: Main Features of the ride-share app that have streamlined the taxi experience.

All features generally apply to both the Driver and Rider apps and user interfaces.

Transportation network companies are able to link drivers and riders through their smartphones, which integrate several software applications and built-in accelerometers, gyroscope, magnetometer and GPS sensors. Today, smartphones are no longer considered a luxury, but a necessity by the 77% of Americans who own them. As a transportation network company, Uber offers services that are primarily powered by software technologies. Artificial intelligence, which is at the core of these technologies, was described by one Uber rider as "Kind of like your boss."

Gone are the days of needing to search through your phone book's Yellow Pages to find local taxi services, calling to set up and waiting impatiently to be picked up.

Ride-hailing companies have taken over and streamlined this process. By utilizing algorithms integrated into software codes powered by AI, they've made the rider experience seem light years away from the unreliable and often unpleasant experience it once was.

Bottom line: you simply need a smartphone with an Internet connection and a downloaded app. You initially set up an account and enter your personal details (home address, billing address, credit card information, and other personal and private information). That's it. You request a ride and your driver arrives within minutes, drives you to your destination and drops you off. Everything else is handled by the middleman: the transportation network company.

An algorithm is a set of rules written to solve a problem(s), and the best is the one that delivers the correct answer in the most efficient manner, far better than any human could. Many algorithms require or collect datasets as they are executed. Machine learning is the computer's ability to read, interpret, and learn from these datasets and make a determination or prediction on their own without further programming, while artificial intelligence refers, in the context of this book, to their ability to learn from such datasets and change algorithms in an "intelligent" manner to mimic or influence human behavioral outcomes.

Storage of these datasets is hierarchical and interconnected with nests of related concepts or decision trees in the same way as the neurons in our brain, forming deep neural networks that can be mined by deep learning. The higher-level features of these deep neural networks are obtained by composing lower-level features. Machines use representation-learning methods that can learn complex functions by transforming data obtained from composing simple but non-linear modules at one level (starting with the raw input) into a representation at a slightly more abstract higher level. Machine learning uses inductive reasoning to make broader inference and prediction of a particular assigned task. Deep learning is therefore a subset of machine learning, which is a subset of AI.

Machine learning tracks your movement (location) and saves the information (data) through the internet to a warehouse (cloud) in some remote location and as you move from place to place, this forms a dataset. AI learns from your past activities by creating a collection of datasets from which it mines data to shape your future behaviors. This process is highly-refined today with deep learning, so the Uber app uses automated processes with less need for low-level tiered human support.

In order to fully appreciate your ride-hailing app and operate it flexibly, you need some basic knowledge of how it was constituted. Uber and other ride-hailing and taxi apps have standard requirements, including an interface that allows both passengers and drivers to register and become members. Another capability allows passengers to book a ride that is matched with drivers who should be able to accept the booking. There are additional abilities to pinpoint a pickup and destination location, a communication platform that links the rider, driver and intermediary transportation network company (if any is involved), a means of determining and calculating pricing and processing payments for such services, and some customer survey or feedback features.

The user interface's flexibility and friendliness vary among the different companies; however, a vital requirement in the back end of these apps is a web administrator server. It collects the histories and statistics of every interaction and saves them as datasets in a database that can be mined to improve their services and help achieve their business goals. This data includes trip information, driver profile and activities (including feedback like ratings or complaints), invoices and earnings data, planned events and activities, and push notifications. Such a viable app should be able to work with both the iOS (iPhone and Mac) and android (Samsung and most others) systems and should be functional for both the customer and the driver.

Understanding that a lot of the processes used by transportation network companies through their app interface are powered by technology, especially artificial intelligence can help both driver and rider regulate certain human decisions that can affect their bottom lines. These apps use integrated geo-locator services like Google Maps, Waze or their own built-in GPS application.

What is the overall advantage of artificial intelligence over human efforts? AI studies a dataset of repeated behaviors and statistics and tries to emulate predictably, with greater efficiency and minimal error, how to perform individual or set of human efforts. The long-term outlook in the world of technology, therefore, is that AI will ultimately replace humans in such activities as driving a car in transportation and logistics, playing games like Chess and Go, or diagnostic and radiographic aids like IBM's Watson computer in healthcare, among others.

Professor Pedro Domingo on KERA's "Think" argues that computer and robots will eventually run all worldly processes due to their efficiency and that humans "will not have to work anymore." I disagree. Just imagine several billion humans in the 22nd Century wandering around idly and aimlessly. I believe the repercussions of such a scenario would give sociologists a lot to discuss and debate.

Here's another way to look at artificial intelligence in these platforms. They compute complex data inputs to particular trip routings to help improve efficiency, but then collect and use additional datasets to take advantage of humans' compulsive and impulsive weaknesses and manipulate our behaviors to follow certain preferred outcomes. You might have some control over how the overall experience rewards you but such control can be compounded by incentives such as money. The machine makes decisions as to the nature and value of any such benefit. Uber uses "data visualization," artificial intelligence, machine learning and other technologies to observe historical trends and match them with current usage patterns to conduct both long-form and real-time prediction.

Uber's Keith Chen on NPR's "Hidden Brain" stated that the company does have access to a tremendous amount of data and, as a result, employs a Privacy Officer.

He added that employees are cautioned to be careful about making queries into individuals' data.

That leads me to question the nature of the "privacy" terms and conditions that we surrender our lives to. They are carefully crafted, often in fine print, as are rules and obligations the end user must abide by before they can utilize the service. They typically specify certain requirements, liabilities, limitations or restrictions, dates or timeline, as well as guidelines for participation. Buried in this contract are carefully-worded disclaimers masked as privacy statements that essentially allow companies to generate, save, mine and deploy our datasets in order to manipulate our lives.

Consider the privacy statement in fine print that tells you that your data is being collected but will not be sold, shared or used carelessly. The extent of these statements vary across different companies. Cookies or plug-ins used for functionality track and collect data. So, what are these personal bits of collected data and how are they accessed?

According to JISAR (March 2018 edition), one or all of the following unique identifiers might be targeted: your iPhone's UDID (Unique Device Identifier), UIDevice object, and your browser of choice (panopticlick.eff.org). Developers can integrate through the UIDevice object to "determine the assigned name of the device, device model and iOS version, orientation (orientation property) of the device, battery charge (batteryState property) and distance of the device to the user (proximityState property)."

Their privacy statement alerts users of two types of information gathering: the ones you provide and the ones they collect. Collected information includes: "location, contacts, transactions, usage and preference, device information, call and SMS data and log information." This gives Uber the ability to publish its own list of the world's most popular attractions. New York City's Empire State Building tops the 2018 list, which covers all six human inhabited continents. That should give you an idea of the breadth of Uber's tentacles.

Do you know that Uber can tell when your cellphone's battery is running low? According to Uber's Chen, the company accidentally learned that more people were willing to tolerate surge pricing once their battery level hit 5% but haven't exploited that knowledge to their advantage. If you're an Uber drive, you might like to know that while you're driving with Google Maps running (even in the background), "Uncle Google" knows everywhere you go? Just go to Google Timeline and you'll see a report that tracks your every move, which is just mind boggling.

Uber took a major step to protect customer privacy in 2018 by removing the street addresses of their pickup and drop-off locations after completion of the ride. The result: drivers can no longer pinpoint the rider's exact address by looking back at the server records they have access to. All they see is the street name of these locations.

Uber knows every location I drive to, whether I am online or offline, and they know the same about riders. The company once camouflaged the ride-hailing app from Apple's engineers such that it secretly identified and tagged iPhones even after its app had been deleted and the device wiped, thus violating Apple's privacy guidelines. Apple CEO Tim Cook forced an end to the practice in a 2015 meeting with then Uber CEO Travis Kalanick, when he threatened to drop the Uber app from Apple's App Store.

With 65,000 organizations around the world using Uber for Business to procure transportation services for their employees and customers, as well as food delivery services through UberEats, Uber knows which restaurants you frequent or order from. They may already have access to all your friends and contacts. Add to that other third party data from apps like Unroll.me that scan a user's inbox and if found, sells any service receipts from competing companies.

Uber can track and manipulate our behaviors in real-time. Research shows that such activities can greatly influence spending behavior in contemporary Western and particularly American society. So it's not a stretch to say that Uber is becoming an advertising company similar to "Uncle Google" who shows me anything I search "...near me" and the omnipresent Facebook, which still tracks you even if you no longer use it because you still use WhatsApp or Instagram. When I read that Uber was rumored to be working on staffing solutions through Uber Works, it did not surprise me. After all, the company can mine real-time information about events and traffic by monitoring partner and rider datasets.

The reason Uber dominated the ride-hailing space despite not having pioneered it isn't hard to figure out. The versatility of its engineers and technology combined with its co- founder and former CEO Travis Kalanick's drive to win almost brought the company down after a string of scandals and negative media attention between 2016 and 2017. Uber even customized my car with "wings" in the visual sent to a potential rider. When I arrived to drive her to DFW International Airport, she showed me the "Batman Car." That's how well Uber can customize its technology.

Other common technologies associated with ride-sharing are car accessories which may include in-car cameras. Texas allows drivers to have a camera in their cars that records every activity without the other party's consent. The passenger can legally do the same.

CHAPTER 4

FOLLOWING THE MONEY, *Literally*

The title of this chapter speaks for itself. I literally had to "follow the money" to make ride-sharing a profitable venture for me. During my first year driving for Uber and Lyft in 2017, I made more than $70,000 in fewer than eight months driving close to 100,000 miles (160,934.4 km) and transported more than 3,000 passengers in the Dallas-Fort Worth Metroplex. I completed 4,500 trips in two calendar years. The most money I made in a single day driving for Uber was $514.31 (St. Patrick's Day on March 17, 2018) and the most in one week was $1,894.16.

Such numbers are only made possible by surge pricing and mine are certainly not the norm. The average Uber or Lyft driver in 2017 reported average hourly earnings of $15.68, according to The Rideshare Guy. A 2015 Princeton study put that value at $19.04 per hour across 20 of Uber's largest U.S. markets, while a 2019 Stanford/Uber study estimated gross hourly earnings of $21.07 for all U.S. drivers between January 2015 and March 2017. In 2018, the average hourly earnings of Uber ride-share drivers in the United States was $14.74 for zero to 500 trips. The 2017 median pay for taxi drivers, ride-hailing drivers and chauffeurs was $24,880 per year ($11.96 per hour) according to the US Bureau of Labor and Statistics. There is some evidence that in 2013 and 2014, Uber drivers may have worked fewer hours yet made more money per hour than the average taxi driver.

According to a 2018 Economic Policy Institute paper, Uber driver compensation—the income after Uber fees and vehicle expenses—averaged $11.77 an hour. Note that $10.87 an hour is the discretionary compensation after mandatory extra Social Security/Medicare taxes, meaning driver earnings are well below the $32.06 average hourly compensation of private-sector workers. The wage further drops down to $9.21 an hour when compared to regular W-2 employees, less than what 90% of workers earn. Lyft claims driver median wage per hour of $18.83 (while online) or $29.47 (at 100% utilization rates) nationwide, and $21.08 (while online) or $31.18 (at 100% utilization rates) per hour in top 25 markets before expense for taxes, gas, car maintenance, etc. of about $3 to $5 per hour.

It is worth noting that at 100% utilization rates which includes intervals when the driver has accepted a trip but has to drive a distance to pick up the rider, a distance that can vary considerably, the driver does not earn a wage for that effort up until they hit a threshold (10 minutes for Uber) after which they eventually earn a fraction calculated from set standard rates. And such additional VMT even though captured, does not get reported by these TNCs when they report annual VMTs. Uber reported consumer VMT.

Uber data from 2013 and 2014 show that although two-thirds of Uber partners were employed full-time before joining, only 8% were fully unemployed when they signed up and 51% had never driven for money before. While most Uber partners don't see driving on the platform as a full-time job, 38% of Uber partners worked full-time on the platform, 31% drove during their spare time from their full-time jobs, and 30% said they held another part-time job. In Uber's 20 largest markets, 80% of its partners drove fewer than 35 hours a week, more than half worked 1 to 15 hours each week and averaged more than $19 an hour in earnings, compared to $12.90 in average hourly wages for cab drivers. Twenty-five percent of drivers were paid $21 to $25 per hour according to an independent study, which also found that 1.5% of drivers earned less than the $7.25 per hour U.S. federal minimum wage. Tracking Uber driver wages is challenging, given how carefully the company guards its data.

I earned well above this range in 2017 but dropped significantly below it in 2018. The drop was consistent with wages for ride-sharing drivers falling by 53% from

2013 to 2017, making it clear that Uber and Lyft drivers are working more and making less.

Two common earnings questions often asked of ride-sharing drivers are:

"Is it worth it?"

"Do you make good money?"

So many riders want to know how much their Uber drivers make, if the Uber gig is worth quitting their job for or adding as part-time activity for extra income. And my most common response to these questions is:

"It depends on your strategy."

Part of my strategy was setting up an UberSelect option that pays higher for rides and obtaining a TollTag from The North Texas Tollway Authority for fast-flowing, less congested, high speed limit tollways, as well as TollPerks Points that can be redeemed for valuable vouchers and prizes, including free offers from favorite local brands. I also recommend having a second phone to act as an extra eye to follow the money in real time.

All ride-sharing drivers need a comprehensive understanding of the geography of their locality and notable hot spots with high probability for rides, the best time of day, specific calendar days and social events, as well as history of ride earnings. I usually drive to or near the target zone before going online, increasing the probability that I get rides from the area. The overnight shift has less traffic congestion, while weekend nights and early mornings have increased ridership from people returning home and others heading to the airport.

Familiarity with ride selection and certain cancellations based on supply and demand of riders and drivers, price jumps, and presence or absence of surge zones is also essential to your strategy. Triaging rider request in a surge zone can help significantly increase your earnings. Wisely managing which rides to accept and which ones to cancel, the distance and time to the pickup location, profiling passenger names, gender and their account type, surge type and my location within the graded zone, or simply calling the passenger are all useful strategies in helping a ride-sharing driver follow the money. Rides with multiple stops popularized in UberPOOL slow down cash flow.

Uber's future, at least in the near term, is heavily dependent on the dynamic pricing Uber was already using. It's getting more experimentation with new CEO Dara Khosrowshahi, who is considered to be an expert, having successfully employed the practice as CEO of Expedia. Dynamic pricing, also referred to as surge pricing, demand pricing, or time-based pricing is a pricing strategy that takes effect when a lot of people in the same area request rides at the same time. This means that rides will be more expensive. Adjusting the price attracts more driver-partners to an area so everyone gets a ride. Customers can wait a few minutes while more driver-partners get on the road, or pay a little extra to get a ride when they need it. Their app notifies them if fares are higher than normal.

Before I ever started studying economics as a subject and understanding its principles in middle school, I had been practicing it in my mother's shop for years growing up and selling every day. We took advantage of basic demand and supply concepts as we scrambled for customers among fierce competitors in the main market. We factored customer behavior into real-time pricing and our only rule was respecting the cost price and ensure a reasonable markup upwards of 33%. A customer with a friendly attitude and little to no knowledge of the product was easy prey. We treated other referred customers and those familiar with the product with care and courted them aggressively.

Here's a good example of our strategy. I make you an offer for a product and you decide to check with my competition. You return later and I notice some extra interest in that same product. I can reasonably assume that I have the better product or my competition was out of it and I never removed any additional discounts and in some cases increased the price. I also increased the price if any of my colleagues in the market took the product from me to sell after a customer had visited my shop for the same product.

These were the same techniques we used when we bought from our suppliers in the commercial capitals in Cameroon, Nigeria and Benin Republic. An introduction by another buyer known to the supplier meant the customer received a discounted price. Claiming knowledge of the market and different suppliers also encouraged sellers to court buyers by offering further discounts. Expert maneuvering can earn the same attractive prices given to volume buyers even when purchasing a single item. These same principles can be used by savvy buyers to force a discount when buying perishable goods, since seller is most likely to sell than take home. Durable goods sellers today also discount certain products like seasonal or returned items to clear space in their shops or avoid logistics and reprocessing overhead costs in the case of returns.

Fast forward to the 21st century. Those techniques have been integrated into AI-run pricing systems called dynamic pricing, surge pricing, demand pricing or time-based pricing. They feature the exponential capability of processing huge amounts of customer behavioral data like shopping experiences and preferences, online trails, video camera logs, financial and spending habits, environmental or geographic factors, and herd or community behaviors that exploit similar inputs.

Long before Uber, the airline industry had mastered and normalized dynamic pricing in air ticketing systems as the price for vacation flights rose with the approach of high demand season. So did the hospitality industry with bookings and reservation of hotels and resorts, and stores like Walmart, where people's zeal to pay less makes their impulses and compulsion vulnerable to manipulation. Amazon is such a master of dynamic pricing in ecommerce that the Federal Trade Commission has investigated the company's deceptive pricing practices.

Uber's dynamic pricing depends on machine learning algorithms that sense demand and supply variations and recruit drivers to high demand areas by raising prices in those areas. The monetary incentive pushes a herd of drivers to those specific locations. It is automatically activated by algorithms that detect real time shifts in consumer demand and driver supply, and because those change constantly, prices get updated every few minutes and can increase or decrease, sometimes significantly. The company claims its machine learning technologies lower rider wait times and increase availability and reliability for riders by smoothing and matching the supply and demand curves. This means that

Uber uses surge pricing to make sure that drivers are always available in areas where a lot of customers need rides.

I've often abandoned other projects to pursue a surge zone, literally following the money. And as I follow the surge, Uber's tracking algorithm recognizes when I approach the periphery of the surge zone and the zone starts to clear up as I enter it. On the app,

I can see a peripheral bleaching effect on the conspicuous red-colored surge zone as the arrow that represents my car on the map enters it. As the surge zones clears, the surge pricing decreases dramatically and even disappears in many cases.

Logically, it makes sense that as a driver on the supply side, entering a high demand area should trigger a dynamic adjustment of the scarcity in supply to reflect my presence and possibly that of other drivers who may be entering the surge zone at the same time. However, there is also the real possibility that I might be the only driver entering a surge zone and if my presence alone can trigger a dramatic drop in the advertised surge price, then Uber certainly manipulated me to get to a high demand area and unfairly decreased or removed the incentive that triggered my chase of the surge pricing. I actually believe that Uber customizes its surge pricing algorithm and manipulates drivers individually. The collective response of these drivers generates a herd behavioral pattern that Uber's algorithms can exploit in future demand and supply mismatches in that particular market. Many veteran drivers I have talked to simply do not chase surge zone heat maps anymore.

On many occasions while within a surge zone, I've declined smaller rates in the hope of getting a rate that is closer to the highest advertised. I don't mind admitting that I've banged on my steering and yelled to myself after spending significant time within a surge zone with no ride while seeing it disappear leaving the regular rate. Occasionally I have simply returned home in frustration, declining the several rides that come in at standard rates. This is how machine learning and AI can manipulate and leave you frustrated.

These behavioral components compound any analysis of variations in demand and labor supply and Uber takes advantage of behavioral economics to match or smooth its demand and supply curves.

Herd behavior refers to "everyone doing what everyone else is doing, even when their private information suggests doing something quite different" (Banerjee, 1992). These individuals retain their autonomy and are not obliged by community policies. They are forced to abandon their personal instincts through fear of group psychology. The community may penalize their behavior as estranged when they fail as outliers but may accommodate or forgive a failure when the individual pursued the general trend.

Such behavior may also just be in response to community behaviors like animal mating norms. This occurs in the Safari, where zebras attempting to migrate to their mating ground continue to try crossing the crocodile-infested Mara River even as they see their comrades fall prey to the reptiles. The hippopotamuses in the river and the predatory lions on the river banks trying to feed on the herd do not deter them either. The urge to do as others is the fear that they may have some information that you are lacking. However, by so many members of the herd abandoning their own information, herd behavior can lead to a "reduction of informativeness.

Uber exploits herd behavior when it makes me chase surge pricing even when I know it may be gone by the time I get there. Once in surge zones the prices are dynamic and I often chase a higher surge and may cancel a previously accepted ride to get a better paying one if the rate increased further.

A higher level analysis of human instincts involved in herd behavior decisions should reveal unique impulsive and compulsive underpinnings that make each community member of the herd go against private information that may have validated a contrarian view or conclusion. TNCs may also indirectly benefit from such "follow-follow" behavioral techniques in their unending driver recruitments and explosive growth in ride-share usage. They gain overall growth through the influx of newcomers, given the high attrition rates in drivers especially, but also riders. By identifying certain characteristics of riders and drivers who become active users, they can exploit herd behaviors and financial enticements like sign-up and referral bonuses to continue recruiting new drivers.

The Uber price surge is an enticement to rally drivers to a high demand area where supply is short. The high demand area is shaded in red color whose intensity increases almost proportionately with the surge factor. The higher the surge, the more alarming and captivating is the red. Uber's new arithmetic surge's dramatization of the red-colored heat maps seem out of proportion with the surge value. A really alarming red-colored heat map can be seen at $4.75 surge. However, in their previous geometric surge system a surge zone of similar red color intensity may have a surge value of 4.8x which will earn the driver several times more for equivalent trips. We know Uber has done a lot of work on its graphical user interface (GUI) but in this case, the difference in red color intensity with lower monetary value is a clear effort to manipulate and rally drivers into high demand areas.

As Uber continues to experiment with surge pricing, the surge area is usually graded such that the highest demand is in the middle and has the highest price surge value, which decreases as you radiate away from this core to much smaller values in the periphery of the defined locales when geometric surge was in place. In my experience with their new arithmetic surge, the gradation of the surge zone pricing has been such that the highest surge price is shifted off to some corner of the zone's periphery, not necessarily that with the highest ride demand. Drivers are naturally pulled toward a high paying pool of riders but the rapidly-changing dynamic nature of the surge, which sometimes changes or even disappears within minutes of the driver's arrival, makes for an impulsive and compulsive response to any of its moving parts. The driver fears missing out on the earnings potential, especially if he/she was lured from home or from an important activity. The compulsion may be linked to opportunity costs, which for me are weighted heavily by my background and skills. I always become annoyed when I'm lured away from another project and end up not making any money.

Such engineered behavior in contemporary American society pulls consumers towards buying things that were not planned just because they're cheap. The same behavior also pulls Uber drivers towards any area where there is a high likelihood of making more money for the same work and effort. Uber's consumer data according to Keith Chen, contradicts 2017 Nobel Prize Winner Richard Thaler's economic theory of mental accounting under surge pricing conditions. Mr. Thaler had witnessed New York City taxi drivers going home after attaining their daily mental earning target (mental accounting) on rainy days, which was easily achieved through high demand and driver supply scarcity.

Uber's Chen, in a 2017 study, showed similar mental account related behavior from Uber drivers with a negative correlation between payout per minute and the share of drivers working. Payouts are high in periods where drivers have higher reservations wages and choose not to drive. Chen did argue on NPR's "Hidden Brain" in 2016 surge pricing entices drivers to increase the length of their work shifts.

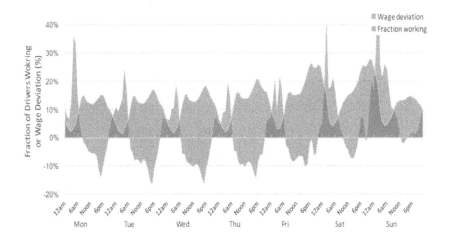

Fig. 7: Wage Deviations vs. Fraction of Time Worked by Uber drivers. (Chen et al., 2017). Printed with Permission.

Wage deviations in Uber's driver pool shows the company's use of surge pricing during low driver supply, the highest and most sustained being on weekend bar closing hours and early Monday mornings propelled by airport ride requests. This is consistent with my experience as a driver.

I prefer driving on high-demand rainy days when Uber surges prices. The bigger and long-lasting the surge, the longer I keep working and often end that shift only after intolerable fatigue, sleepiness, or if the mandatory 12-hour driving limit logs me off. Uber's Chen argues this is the result of monetary enticement from the surge and I agree. However, I always have a mental account target or reference point for each day I leave home to drive for Uber. In 2017, that daily target was at least $150 per day, although I usually shot for $250. So, even if the weather improved and the surge disappeared, I still worked until I made $150. If the weather persisted and the surge continued, I worked until I made $250 and continued beyond that attainment level until I grew too tired to keep driving. So I continued to drive beyond my mental accounts.

Cash is my motivation on bad weather days and I keep following the high paying ride requests as they come in until eventually my body reaches its breakpoint. The high availability of these rides puts me in a more relaxed state of mind and less likely to have impulsive reactions when in dynamic, fast-changing surge zones. By continuing to work during a sustained surge, I am able to have more downtime and flexibility to pursue other areas of my life. This is contrary to Mr. Thaler's assertions on NPR's "Hidden Brain" and is supported by surveys that show that 55% of ride-share (Uber and Lyft) drivers prioritize pay while 35% prioritize flexibility, and 80% or more of Uber drivers value its flexibility of work model. Chen et al. (2017) showed that the main benefit from flexible work is the ability to work only in those hours when reservation wages are lower than expected earnings.

The extra effort for the extra money with the knowledge that I'm on my own is actually a major driving and sustaining force during surging prices in inclement weather (risky conditions).

Uber Wages vs. Minimum Wages in US Cities with the Most Ride-sharing

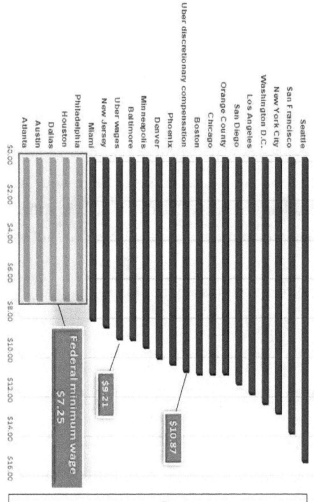

Wages in Cities that Account for 70% of US Ride-sharing

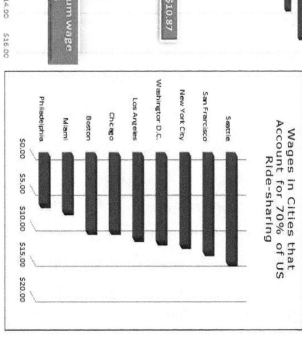

Fig 8: Uber Driver Wages Compared to Minimum Wages.

Based on EPI minimum wage tracker, January 2018 and Schaller Consulting Ride-sharing Analysis. Uber discretionary compensation is $10.87 after paying extra Social Security/Medicare tax of 7.65% paid by self-employed.

Choosing my own schedule is the reason I will still work although I know I might earn less than a surged rate or a prevailing wage because I value other aspects of the job like its accommodation to positive shocks (stop work when child is sick) or negative shocks (start work to pay unexpected bills). My reservation wage for Uber in the Dallas market is usually $15-$20 an hour but there have been plenty of times I have worked below the $7.25 federal mandated minimum wage. Uber has not shared its prevailing or expected wages for any market and no survey has directly addressed the Dallas market.

Uber's app, with its changing directives and commanding imageries, sends powerful optical sensory information through my eyes to my brain. These may excite different brain neurons and tip over already ongoing spontaneous fluctuations in brain activity into more organized readiness potentials called bereitschaftspotential that compel me to drive according to Uber's commands, even before my mind is ready for these actions.

Sometimes my smartphone rings inside my pocket but as I reach to remove it, any accidental touch of the screen automatically accepts the incoming ride requests and takes away my free will to first observe or verify the details of the incoming call. Even though Uber added a "Decline" option to the incoming ride request screen, the app still takes control of the phone and any touch on the screen automatically accepts that ride request. The "Decline" option is one degree of freedom for the driver to voluntarily opt out of a ride request. Uber eventually got rid of its imposing circular ringing icon that consumed the whole screen of one's smartphone. Now there is a "swipe right" requirement to start or complete a trip with a prompt in scenarios where drivers are likely to make an accidental screen touch.

Dynamic pricing is also customizable such that not all consumers pay the same price for identical items. Given Uber's history of using stealth technologies to study certain groups of people or punish them, I will not be surprised if the company moves in that direction. A 2016 Forbes article raised the specter of Uber targeting customers with low cellphone battery charge with surge pricing since they can detect such state (as admitted by Uber's Head of Economic Research) based on all the information they collect from our phones.

With all this information, Uber even knows if most people prefer a 1.9x surge over a 2.0x surge or a 2.1x surge. Apparently, the integer "2" appears scary in most people's minds, seeming to have a significant value of a doubled price compared to 1.9. Six times more people requested rides at 1.9x surge than 2.0x surge and an even higher number requested rides at 2.1x surge than a 2.0x surge. In my experience, Uber surges are often fractional gradations and rarely integers like 2.0x, 3.0x, 4.0x, etc.

When I started driving for Uber, the price surge was geometric, a multiplier of the regular fare. Although surge pricing continues, Uber switched from a 'geometric' to an 'arithmetic' surge in late 2018, meaning that a fixed extra numeric dollar amount is now added to the regular fare. This is similar to what Lyft Prime Time does, except that with Prime Time, a percentage of the regular fare is calculated and added to the base fare. So a Prime Time of 50% for a ride that normally costs $20 will result in the rider paying $30, where half ($10) is added to the base $20 fare. I would not be surprised if Lyft's research shows that people may tolerate a percentage over a numeric multiplier.

Triaging rider requests in a surge zone can significantly increase driver earnings. If a driver turns on the Uber Driver app and goes online before entering the surge zone, the app will likely find the rider closest to that driver that could be out of the surge zone or on the periphery. So drivers definitely want to turn the app on once they are closest to the core of a surge zone. The surge is always dynamic and may increase but often decreases before drivers get to the core.

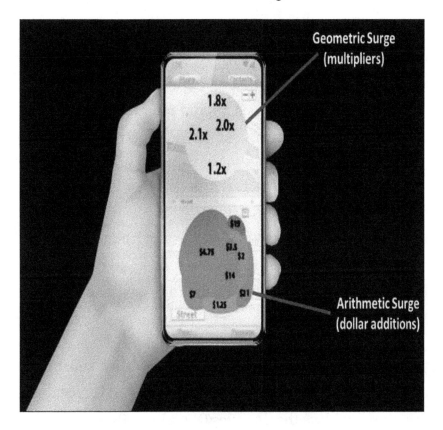

Fig. 9: Surge pricing: Geometric and Arithmetic models.

When I go online as I enter the surge zone, I'm not likely to miss out on getting a request. If I get a smaller surge and can still determine that there is a higher one nearer the core, I keep driving toward the core and cancel the smaller surge. That works in my favor more often than not. Sometimes I drive into the core without getting a ride request even when the surge is still showing on the app. This can be extremely frustrating, especially if I've gone out of my way to reach the surge or left an enjoyable activity in the hope of making money. This has angered me so badly on occasion that people heard me screaming inside the car. Simply refreshing the app several times or uninstalling and reinstalling it fixes the issue although the surge may have expired by the time the app is working properly again. Sometimes an app malfunction or freeze might affect driver account status and restrict going back online.

Many times during a price surge, I only get incoming ride requests without any surge at all. A similar message may appear if I selectively seek only UberSelect rides and don't get one for a long time, or if under UberX I decline too many trips or cancel too many accepted rides.

Uber's arithmetic surge is excellent for short trips and is worth something only when they are high, sustained, frequent, and less than 5 miles (8.05 km). However, since the Uber surge is dynamic, it often does not last long and expert drivers like me end up with just a fraction of our regular earnings. As a driver, my bold prediction is that geometric surge will eventually be brought back. Otherwise, as Mr. Chen argued, Uber will alienate and eventually lose the most dependable drivers who keep the company's revenue stream predictable. It is worth noting that "the flexibility of work schedule and higher compensation rates are among the main reasons Uber is attractive to drivers."

It is a hybrid of both systems at different times within the same market or across different markets based on the volumes of behavioral data.

Bottom line: dynamic pricing is here to stay, at least at Uber. Surge pricing has been an integral part of the company's success, according to its Head of Economic Research at the time, Keith Chen on NPR's Hidden Brain. He also asserts in that interview that Uber's fares are up to 60% lower than taxi fares when the price is not surging in many major U.S. cities. He argues that the company tries to balance advertising such cheap rates as discounts, which makes customers happy but tends to alienate drivers.

In my experience, surge pricing helps drivers make more money while helping Uber gross more revenue by taking a significant cut of price increases. Mr. Chen argues that the reason Uber drivers make more than taxi drivers is constantly having a paying rider in the back seat. However, I can attest that on many occasions I have driven for several hours with Uber and made less than the federal minimum wage per hour before expenses. I once circulated for almost two hours in late 2018 and had one ride that paid me $2.85. Believe it or not, that wasn't my worst payday ever! Such low utilization rates and deadheading to pick-up locations compound the Uber driver earnings picture and further exposes them to surge pricing manipulations.

I feel that Uber should either standardize its rates or simply emulate taxi rates. Much of this feeling stems from my frustrations in chasing dynamic surges that do not reflect the earnings expectations Uber advertised. Surge pricing is an entrapment to ride-share drivers, whose compulsive dependence on a wage leaves them vulnerable to psychological manipulation. Once they're lured to the high demand surge area and Uber removes the surge pricing, they must accept the regular price or make no money, even after investing time, effort and cost of operating a car. Moreover, Banerjee et al. (2015) showed that the performance (throughput and revenue) of dynamic pricing at best, optimizes static pricing though it is also much more robust to fluctuations in system parameters compared to static pricing. I believe that its manipulative exploitation of drivers who incur operational and opportunity costs in efforts pursuing surging prices is a problem in the current business models of TNCs.

These TNCs on the other hand, use surge pricing as more of a manipulative tool when targeting their consumers. These customers' savings potential is more impulsive than compulsive, with options to wait for the surge pricing to drop, try another ride-share service, or take a taxi or shuttle. Most ride-sharing drivers agree that surge pricing entraps them beyond simple manipulation, and they may end up making less or losing money after chasing the surge for miles. Many who share my experiences simply choose not to pursue surge pricing, or are more strategic in pursuing those that are more likely to be sustained, such as rides following big events.

Uber knows that consumers feel less entrapped during surge pricing than drivers. It also knows that riders are sensitive to these price hikes, especially their numerical multiplicative increments, as was the case with geometric surge pricing. That knowledge prompted the company to switch to the more covert, highly complicated and less intimidating arithmetic surge pricing. For short trips, the numeric dollar amounts added are straightforward but Uber makes a proprietary adjustment on certain long trips that renders the arithmetic surge far more expensive to the rider.

An independent study by Kooti et al. (2017) using Uber billing emails found that drivers who take advantage of surge pricing can earn on average 60% more, while working the same number of hours. I should note, however, that this study was conducted during the era of geometric surge pricing. Uber's dynamic pricing has worked for me and played a significant role in my ability to make a lot of money as a ride share driver in 2017. Uber cites the best evidence for its surge algorithm's effectiveness as its remarkable consistency in reducing the expected wait time for a ride with a driver almost always fewer than five minutes away, since the surge pricing encourages an increased supply of drivers, thus smoothing or matching the demand and supply curve. The company also acknowledges the benefit of surge pricing to driver earnings.

However, its covert manipulation of drivers may eventually become counterproductive given high driver attrition rates. Only 4% of people who sign up to drive are still driving a year later, reports The Information. A Stanford/Uber study on the other hand found that number to be close to 70%. Some 17% of ride-share drivers say they drive for Lyft only, with 76% being "satisfied with their experience." Compare that to 69% who drive for Uber only, with 58% being "satisfied" while 20% of drivers drive for both companies according to The Rideshare Guy's survey of more than one thousand drivers in 2018. Lyft spent 37% ((calculated as 804/2157) x 100%) on sales and marketing in 2018 to retain drivers and riders on the platform compared to Uber's 28% ((calculated as 2151/11270) x 100%). That's not what we expect to see from an emerging 'tech company'.

I also believe that Uber's transition from geometric to arithmetic surge pricing must be in response to internal data from comprehensive studies. The company knows that riders eventually accept surged prices despite initial indignation, registered as a 27% decrease in ride requests that over time drops to just 7% after people become accustomed to the concept of surge pricing. They may have additional data that's worse or perhaps the use of the arithmetic surge is a behavioral containment of riders' immediate instinct to not request rides at surging prices.

Not surprisingly, Amazon is already making significant moves into the logistics sector, while quietly expanding its network of driver partners and airline fleet. Now the world's biggest e-commerce company, Amazon (AMZN) took advantage of positive media coverage in 2018 and awarded its second headquarters (HQ2) location to Crystal City, Virginia and Long Island City, New York. This followed a 14-month challenge that received applications from 238 cities, each of which basically surrendered its future planning and strategies to a privately-owned company for free. This gave Amazon executives the ability to plan into the future with privileged knowledge of the strategic vision of some of the biggest cities in North America.

When the company launched its search for a second headquarters, many cities across North America (the majority in the United States) were lured by the promise of some 50,000 high-paying jobs and all the development that historically accompanies such gigantic human and capital flow. The winning bids surrendered more than $9 billion in tax breaks to Amazon, which exploited herd behavior and maximized opportunities to not pay taxes given up by these cities even when it was to the detriment of the broader community and nation. Some political opportunist leaders in New York City and widespread negative media attention eventually forced Amazon to withdraw its headquarter plans for New York in February 2019.

Amazon Flex is the company's program that partners with drivers in the same way Uber and Lyft do, but only delivers Amazon products, which helps the company fulfill such promises as same-day, one-day and two-day deliveries. Once active on the Amazon Flex platform, drivers must go to the app and click on available delivery offers before they can be sure of a job for that day or week. In the Dallas-Fort Worth area, the competition for these jobs is fierce and on several occasions I have spent several minutes or even hours just staring at, and swiping on my phone in search of published job offers. Many often appear in the mornings but the probability of success is slim, given the hundreds or thousands of drivers all swiping to win that same job offer.

The psychological impact of artificial intelligence on herd behavior can be seen in real time but the neuro-developmental or synaptic regenerations or reformations will bear out over several years. The ride-sharing driver will be one of the best pool of subjects where such evolution can be studied, given their dependence on the remuneration and the consequent compulsive expulsion that leaves them vulnerable to AI manipulation. Due to loss aversion or fear of missing out on the high paying surge once within the surge zone, ride-share drivers are very susceptible to being manipulated.

A study of London taxi drivers' brains showed asymmetrical ballooning of the hippocampus with excellence in memory and declining cognitive skills. What will similar or comparative brain studies of AI-manipulated ride-share drivers show, especially on modulation of free will and self-control?

CHAPTER 5

TRUE COST OF A RIDE

In the quarter that ended December 31, 2018, Uber announced that the average fare for a ride-sharing trip was under $9.00. While a typical Uber driver makes $24.77/hour from trip payments by riders, Uber's cut of $8.33 in commissions and fees leaves their drivers at the edge of minimum wage when gas and car maintenance cost of about $4.87/hour is removed. A short Uber ride of a mile or two in the Dallas market usually pays the driver about $2.85 when the rider is charged about $6 or sometimes less. Imagine a 17-minute drive (17 min x $0.12 = $2.04) at 35 mph (56.33 km/h) to pick up a rider 10 miles (16.09 km) away (10 mi x $0.6 = $6.0) for a shopping trip that lasts a few minutes. The Uber driver ends up losing money on almost half an hour of his/her day's work. Since Uber instituted a Long Pickup Fee, I generally get some payment for any distance travelled after the first 10 minutes which from my experience is usually less than a dollar. The company also makes a "Min Fare Supplement" on very short rides to bring those fares to $2.85 in the Dallas market.

Back in early 2017 when I started driving for Uber, the company charged $0.6375/mile, and $0.0750/minute of wait-time or time driven for UberX. The per mile charge was increased to $$0.6825 by mid-year as Uber rolled out its 180 Days of Change campaign to better relations with its driver partners. Uber VIP used these rates but UberSelect in late 2017 was paying $1.4325/mile and $0.1875/minute for time driven and $0.2400/ minute for wait-time. In July 2018, UberX and VIP paid $0.6000/mile, $0.1200/minute for time driven and $0.2100/minute for wait-time, while UberSelect paid $0.9000 /mile and $0.4875/minute for wait-time or time driven.

The airport rider fee in 2019 is $3.0. On its blog, Uber said they were "increasing the per-minute rate and decreasing the per-mile rate for UberX, UberPool, and UberXL.

Whether it's a 2-mile trip or a 20-mile trip, your time will be valued" and that they were "putting more value on time to help create more consistent and dependable earnings, no matter where your next trip takes you".

Take an UberX trip that traveled 10 miles (16.09 km) in 15 minutes with 2 minutes of wait time. In early 2017 such a trip paid $7.65 (10 x $0.6375 + 15 x $0.0750

+ 2 x $0.0750 = $7.65). In early 2019, the same trip pays $8.04 (10 x $0.6 + 15 x $0.1200 + 2 x $0.1200 = $8.04). This represents a 5.1% increase for this short trip in the new system.

However, consider an UberX airport trip that traveled 30 miles (48.28) in 30 minutes with two minutes of wait time. In early 2017, such a trip paid $21.5 (30 x $0.6375 + 30 x $0.0750 + 2 x $0.0750 = $21.5). In early 2019, the same trip pays $21.84 (30 x $0.6 + 30 x $0.1200 + 2 x $0.1200 = $21.84). This represents a 1.6% increase for this long trip in the new system.

Uber's increased commission means the company takes more from rider payments in 2019 than it took in 2017, and the driver ends up with lower earnings now than they did in 2017. As a consequence, I have noticed that for the same trips between two fix points, say from DFW International Airport and a Downtown Dallas hotel, my earnings have steadily decreased from early 2017 to early 2019.

So to an extent, Uber has increased the value of its drivers' time in the new payment system, which means taking longer to drop a rider, or simply being inefficient may earn the driver a bit more. This is also the case for Long Pickup Fee where drivers can simply delay until after the 10-minute threshold to receive a fee in long distance pickup requests. I still believe that ride-sharing per-mile rates have to go up and surpass the per-mile cost of running a vehicle and also be consistent with the services provided by these extraordinary partner drivers.

One of my highest advertised geometric price surges was a 4.8x, which gave me an extra $60.07 for a trip total of $76.73. My highest geometric price surge ever was a 5.9x for a short trip. My highest advertised arithmetic price surge was +$21 for a 4.11 mile (6.61 km), 10 minute trip that paid a total of $25.42. A breakdown of the fare receipts for these surges show that with geometric surges, riders pay the whole bill and Uber receives a commission but with the arithmetic surges, there is a rider promotion and a service fee adjustment that lands Uber's cut in the negative for short trips. However, high surging long trips are dramatically more expensive for riders and both Uber and the driver make significantly more than with a geometric surge.

My biggest Uber surge earning from DFW International Airport was a 3.0x geometric surged ride from the airport to southwest Fort Worth, where I dropped off a gas engineer. It was a +$20 ride that paid me a total of $48.28 for the surge after Uber made "an adjustment to ensure that I receive a significant portion of the rider surge price." The rider paid $124.95 for a 28.35 mile (45.62 km), 28 minute and 36 second trip, from which my total earning was $69.77 and Uber's cut was $55.18 (service fee of $52.33 and booking fee of $2.85). Uber reported charges for base fare as $0.75, for distance as $17.01 (at $0.6000/mi), for time as $3.43 (at $0.1200/min), and for wait time as $0.30 (at $0.2100/min). This brings the total charge for this ride without any surge to $21.49. Therefore, if this same ride surged at a geometric 5.0x ("applies to base, distance and time") and we used the $21.19 ($0.75 + $17.01 + $3.43) to calculate what it would have cost the rider, he would have paid $105.95, which is still less than the $124.99 this rider paid.

Only Uber knows what adjustments it made to this trip to ensure that I received a significant portion of the rider surge price. In its calculation of its TAM and SAM, the company uses the following distance cut-offs: <3 miles (4.83 km), 3 miles (4.83 km) — 30 miles (48.28 km), >3 miles (4.83 km). However, in the new arithmetic surge, I have noticed that surge price adjustments only happen in certain long distance trips and the adjustments escalate the price the higher the surge and the longer the distance.

Let's look at some more examples. A 22.49 mile (36.19 km) 24 minute, 14 second trip surged at $4 received no adjustment. An 8.82 mile (14.19 km) 13 minute, 19 second trip surged (arithmetic) at $9.25 received no adjustment. A 38.02 mile (61.19 km) 32 minute, 29 second trip from Deep Ellum to Fort Worth surged at $7.00 received an adjustment of $3.07 for a surge total of $10.09, of which Uber took $29.73 (44.2%) of the $67.29 the rider paid and gave me the other $37.56 (55.82%).

On the other hand, a DFW International Airport outbound 20.26 mile (32.61 km) 21 minute, 19 second trip to Fort Worth surged (arithmetic) at $7.50 received no adjustment and Uber took $1.48 (4.6%) separate from a $3.00 rider fee and gave me $30.83 from the $35.31 the rider paid. This ride definitely gave me my highest cut from any ride since I started ride-sharing. Another DFW International Airport outbound 25.71 miles (41.36 km) 27 minute 13 second trip to Plano surged (arithmetic) at $3.0 did receive an adjustment of $4.05, from which Uber took $21.66 (41%) separate from a $3.0 Rider Fee and gave me $31.27 from the $55.93 the rider paid. A non-airport related trip with $3.0 arithmetic surge took 13 minutes and nine seconds to travel 14.18 miles (22.82 km), received no surge adjustment, and Uber took a $5.31 (28%) commission from the $19.15 the rider paid for the trip.

What these examples show is how difficult it is to understand Uber's surge algorithm and how unpredictable the driver earnings can be. They show that Uber may make adjustments to an arithmetic surge to improve driver earnings, or just reduce its commission to achieve the same effect. Such inconsistency does not only affect driver wages but may also be a long-term problem for Uber as it continues to lose money amid slowing growth.

I offer these examples to demonstrate how Uber has taken control of the dynamic pricing process away from both the rider and the driver. Under the geometric surge system, a 3.0x multiplier could not be significantly different from a simple mathematic process that both the rider and driver could calculate. However, with the current arithmetic surge, a rider can get a quote of $124.95 but will not be able to know how that surge value was determined nor can the driver estimate what he/she will make from the trip. Just more proof of Uber's growing control over both riders and drivers.

I once picked up a rider at 2:41 AM from the Deep Ellum bar district with a 2.0x surge and drove him to his home in McKinney, some 30 miles (48.28 km) away. The trip netted me an extra $25.52 for a trip total of $51.03. This Millennial could have waited 19 minutes to pay regular pricing and save about $20 but there may be other reasons why the young Pacific Northwesterner who'd just moved to the Dallas area and was seriously looking for a girlfriend did not mind the extra cost. While a rider can wait out a price surge, the driver must rush into the surge zone because the price surge is time limited.

Uber fares may vary depending on the city and the selected vehicle option, and trip fares might be calculated upfront or immediately after the ride ends. I have noticed certain inputs used in fare calculation, including a base rate, rates for estimated time and distance of the route, a booking fee and any applicable surcharges, rider fees and tolls, as well as any surge multiplier or addition from dynamic pricing. This means that if an upfront fare is not honored, the rider will either be charged the minimum fare or a higher fare once all inputs are factored. I have never understood when and by whom a rider fee is collected, although I have mostly seen them on airport-related flights. Lyft mentioned a $3.00 airport fee its IPO filing to the Securities and Ex- change Commission, SEC.

As of this book's publication, Uber claimed on its website that it "charges partners a 25% fee on all fares" that covers "the use of Uber software," "collection and transfer of fares," "credit card commission," and "distribution of invoices to clients." Fare details show that for every ride, Uber's cut involves a booking fee and a service fee. Starting in early 2019, Uber charges UberEats drivers on its platform a service fee for every delivery. The company claims the funds will help it "offset increasing operational costs including those related to insurance and background checks." Lyft's cut of 18% in 2016 grew to 27% in 2018. From my experience, Uber's commission per ride typically falls between 35% and 55% and which one the driver gets hit with de- pends exclusively on Uber's discretion or algorithm.

A 3.82 mile (6.15 km) ride that drops off a passenger on the south side of DFW International Airport at United Airlines' luggage services on the service roads charges a $3 rider fee for entering the airport. This ride usually takes about six minutes to complete and I only end up with $3.82 of the $10.65 that the rider usually pays. This clearly leaves me with only a third (about 35%) of the total receipts, with Uber taking about 65%, making these rides the lowest paid during my time driving for Uber.

Assume no rider fee was collected, and the rider ended up paying $7.65. I'd still go home with just 50% of the proceeds. Another ride from this area, dropping off the passenger inside the airport for a total of 5.9 miles (9.5 km) and a duration of 10 minutes and five seconds, paid me $7.53. This included a $2 airport access fee from a total rider quote of $14.10, a discount of $4.23, a $3 rider fee and a rider payment of $9.87. I received $53.4% of the original quote while Uber received -$0.66 due to the discounts it offered the customer.

In my experience, the $3 rider fee usually applies when the rider is picked up or dropped off in or around the airport in areas the company has zoned out. Since an August 2017 Reuters article also questioned Uber's true valuation of a ride, myself I wondered why certain equivalent rides show significant discrepancies in their fares.

Exploiting equivalent Uber rides can help maximize my earnings. I define an equivalent ride as one that leaves or gets dropped off at a location near a previously completed ride pickup or drop-off location and heads to a destination similar to or near a previously completed ride pickup or drop-off location using similar routes. The expectation of such equivalent rides is that the earnings will have few discrepancies. However, in 2017 and the first half of 2018, I noticed and exploited many huge discrepancies among equivalent Uber rides. It wasn't until later in 2018 that I noticed such equivalent rides have little differences in their earnings.

Let me give you an example. Three different riders on three different occasions paid me $28.67, $65.30 and $88.49 respectively, although I followed the same route to the Dallas Love Field Airport for each trip at approximately the same time of day (early morning). I initially attributed these discrepancies to price surges but I finally became suspicious because there were no advertised surges before each ride. Zooming into the details of these fares revealed that the toll always lacks a standardized rate and varies among the rides from $6.66, $46.22 and $68.55 respectively. Rider payments were

$51.90, $40.04 and $35.52 respectively and there were no surge additions in the fare details. The actual toll, as shown from the early January 2019 NTTA account statement in Fig. 10 below, was $3.88.

Transaction Date/ Time	Posted Date/ Time	Lane	Dir	Location	Transaction Type/ Description	Amount
01/30/2019 04:57	01/30/2019 04:59	SRT-COIRD-02	S	Coit Road (COIRD)	Toll	-0.62
01/30/2019 05:02	01/30/2019 05:04	DNT-MLP3-05	S	Parker Main Lane Gantry (MLP3)	Toll	-1.00
01/30/2019 05:05	01/30/2019 05:07	DNT-MLP2-04	S	Trinity Mills Main Lane Gantry (MLP2)	Toll	-1.12
01/30/2019 05:13	01/30/2019 05:15	DNT-MOCLN-01	S	Mockingbird Lane (MOCLN)	Toll	-1.14

Fig. 10: NTTA toll receipt

One factor playing a significant role in these price variation is the type of work the riders do at their company affiliation. Occasional equivalent trips involving business travelers and consultants around the Legacy West area usually pay me more per ride than other travelers, especially those on personal holidays and pleasure trips, when I force a toll dump. This indicates that Uber charges more from companies than from individuals, so I refocused my strategy towards these corporate workers.

An extra $5-$10 dollar per ride for three to four rides a day increases my daily earnings by 15-20% or more, which is equivalent to a geometric surge of about 1.2x. However, a careful analysis of the fare discrepancies in the above three examples of equivalent rides shows Uber received $18.23, -$30.26 and -$52.97 respectively for those rides. Uber only made money in one of those rides and lost money in the other two. From my significant experience driving for Uber I believe that this is not by accident, but is a commission or bonus Uber offers me.

I don't know the company's internal accounting processes but I can see why it is still losing significant amounts of money in order to keep drivers and customers happy. All accounts statements that I have access to are balanced. On the other hand, what if this is actually a glitch in the software codes that's gone unnoticed for at least two years? What if Uber is aware of the problem but has thus far been unable to solve it? I know that at least one other Uber driver f reported making more than $100 per ride from the same vicinity. So how many such errors are made for how many rides across how many cities?

Just before this book's publication, the toll dumps from the Frisco-McKinney area had stopped but I did force another toll dump on a trip from Uptown Dallas to Plano. Uber must address this issue in its early periods as a publicly traded company in 2019.

Uber employees are not trained to properly make toll adjustments. Further, outsourced agents in India typically reply to complaints with the same scripted message. They often use arithmetic algorithm that roughly adds the toll values per gate passed, instead of integrating and summing only the two overhead gates plus that of the entry and exit gates. For any of the three equivalent rides discussed above, they sum the toll values of some or all of the 16 toll booths that cover the trip path to get the total toll for that trip.

The highest toll compensation I've received from an Uber trip also originated from the same area discussed above with a similar destination to Dallas Love Field Airport.

I was paid a record $105.74 following a toll dump I forced from the north entry to the DNT and southbound to Dallas Love Field Airport. The trip total was $130.50, of which the rider paid $44.03 while Uber lost $86.47. I have occasionally received $0 toll compensation, especially for airport routes through TX-121 but I'm usually paid the $2 DFW International Airport access fee.

AI automation of most intermediary TNC processes in the ride-sharing transaction sometimes results in costly code errors. One of these is calculating tolls. Uber expects its drivers to review all rides and submit any missing tolls without delay. I have no way of knowing the exact rate until the NTTA statement is received or every ride is submitted for processing on their website or app, which can take several minutes per ride. Automation code failures require drivers to take on additional responsibilities that reduce efficiency in earning a respectable wage or get bogged down trying to manually process or correct toll transactional differences.

I coined the term "toll dumping" for the confusion in the software's ability to properly recognize route changes that are dependent on the driver, then update or integrate the information to its algorithm and properly calculate tolls for the choosing trip routes. This leads to a manual adjustment after the driver feedback or an automatic dumping of a random toll payment for that trip.

Toll dumping had three outcomes: the first is when it missed picking up the route correctly or wrongly picked up a toll charge due to close proximity. Each time I have taken the I-635 eastbound toll entry just before the intersection with I-35E, the app has not recognized that slight lane change that puts me on the tollway, making it difficult for the software's geo-locator to pick it up. Lyft even charged me a $3 toll when my driver used the access route of DFW International Airport, where I would have been charged an additional $2 or $4 time-based fee if we transited through the airport tollgates.

The second outcome of toll dumping occurs when the software fails to pick up or recognize and pay tolls for a route regularly traveled by me sometimes when I do multiple equivalent rides within the same period on the same day, paying tolls on some. The third outcome, occurs when the software becomes confused because I switch between two toll roads either preprogrammed for the trip or I force or switch to such a route for traffic reasons. Sometimes, it's simply to take advantage of payout that usually accompanies such a toll dump. For instance, I earn more for a ride from around the Virginia Road and Coit Road intersection in McKinney destined to DFW International Airport when I use the Rockhill Pkwy route through to Dallas North Tollway to TX-121 instead of the Coit Road route to TX-121. The difference can be up to $10 or more. My biggest toll dump ever was $105.74.

Affected toll roads and the different intersection on them that once dumped tolls in the DFW Metroplex include where TX-380, Sam Rayburn Tollway (SRT or TX-121), President George Bush Turnpike (PGBT), I-35E and I-635 intersect with the Dallas North Tollway (DNT); where Sam Rayburn Tollway and President George Bush Turnpike intersect with I-35E; and where President George Bush Turnpike intersects with I-635. It is worth mentioning that the overall routes taken in toll dumps rarely significantly altered the total trip distance and similar toll dumping effects were achieved by simply altering local street routes and arterials.

Uber is a cashless experience in most cities. I have seen the option of paying with cash on the rider app but have never used it. On the drivers' side and the ability to access their money, Uber and Lyft make it easy for drivers to collect trip earnings within a few minutes after they are posted. With the Instant Cash or Instant Pay option, the driver can claim all the endings less the $0.50 charge per withdrawal, money which is deposited into their bank account immediately. This is an effective way to make money on the fly driving for transportation network companies because drivers can drive for a few hours and cash out on their earnings. This helps bring in money when it is needed quickly, instead of waiting until the regular weekly payout on the Wednesday following the pay period starting at 4 AM Monday morning of the previous week to 4 AM Monday morning of the new week. Since May 2017, Uber publishes in-app fare details that include the total paid by the rider, the company's cut, and other fees seen in some invoices but not others. Uber sends the rider one billing email receipt for the ride.

The average Uber rider who is a business traveler tips $4.03. This adds to drivers' earnings and, technically anyway, to the true cost of a ride. However, due to the voluntary nature of tips, they cannot be standardized to the drivers' earnings and cost of a ride. Based on my experience and that of a few other drivers I spoke to, Lyft riders are more likely to tip. It's a different story with Uber. There were days I drove up to 21 trips and not received a single tip since the company launched its in-app tipping feature in July 2017.

Both Uber and Lyft use arithmetic tipping, which tips a fixed dollar amount ($1, $2, $4, etc.), while geometric tips a percentage of the final trip cost (5%, 7%, 15%, etc.).

As a driver following the money, an arithmetic format is best for short trips and the geometric model pays better in long-distance trips. TNCs can also use minimum tips on the menu so that a trip costing $5 may show a $1 tip option but a trip costing $50 may have a $5 or $8 minimum tip option.

A similar cut off can be applied with geometric tipping. Riders are currently given an option to customize their tips to whatever value they would like to give. Lyft limits gratuities to $50 or 200% of the cost of the ride, whichever is lower. TNCs may not have any incentive to use their intrusive AI behavioral models to manipulate riders to tip drivers huge amounts because of the cash burden on their customer and 100% of tips from riders go to drivers. No commissions are deducted since a tip is not part of a trip cost.

After introducing in-app tipping, Uber actually pushed back against drivers with published findings that tips did not improve the quality of service and that tipping would impede the hassle-free user experience which was its biggest customer lure.

Following Uber's "180 Days of Change" campaign, the company started charging riders $15 for any lost and found item that is returned to the owner. This adds to the ride's cost and inconveniences riders but was a welcome change to Uber drivers who were previously expected to return recovered items to riders or drop them at an Uber Greenlight Hub. They were not compensated for their time, effort and cost of operating their vehicles to perform this courtesy service. That campaign also improved on cancellation rates from riders, before which some days up to 50% of my requests were cancelled. In-app tipping was also introduced in July 2017 with Uber matching rider tips in those early days.

I never received a sign-on bonus to become an Uber partner, but I've definitely benefitted from the company's commissions. The true cost of a ride is sure to change but ride-share companies will have to be more transparent with their surge pricing data and model, charge for each ride proportionately to the cost of operating a vehicle, and standardize and reduce their commissions. This will ensure that drivers doing the end-user operation and bearing the driving risks receive the most money.

CHAPTER 6

COST TO COMMUNITIES AND BUSINESSES

Schaller Consulting estimates 70% of Uber and Lyft trips occur in nine large U.S. metropolitan areas and in eight of these (except New York), and they account for 90% of taxi rides totaling 5.7 billion additional miles of driving annually (in Boston, Chicago, Los Angeles, Miami, New York, Philadelphia, San Francisco, Seattle and Washington DC metro area).

Local communities are, therefore, key stakeholders in the shared economy, especially in the area of ride-sharing services. Some towns and cities embrace these technology- driven innovative companies. Others oppose them, going so far as passing legislation to restrict their presence or ban them altogether. New York City became the face of the protests with its powerful taxi and limousine industry trying to keep transportation network companies (especially Uber) from entering the city. Taking the opposite stance, Texas passed 2017 legislation limiting the power of local communities to restrict or control TNC's activities, thereby upending cities like Austin.

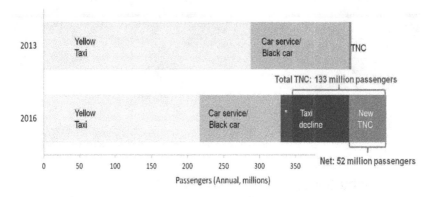

Fig. 11: Number of Passengers NYC, 2013 and 2016. (Schaller Consulting). Printed with permission

Note the drop in Taxi ridership.
* Trip requests made through TNC apps and dispatched to drivers affiliated with black car and car service bases.

Local law enforcement, including city police, county sheriffs, state troopers and rangers, emergency personnel and other regulatory and security officers are charged with overseeing ride-sharing operations. In addition to their other duties, they enforce ride-sharing violations in the areas of airport-specific car sticker permits, parking, traffic flow, curbside restrictions, passenger solicitation, as well as zoning restrictions in the waiting areas and passenger pickup activities.

In 2000, 50% of peak-hour travel occurred under congested conditions, with urban interstates cited as the most crowded. Researchers estimated that in 1999, the annual lost productivity costs resulting from congestion-related delays were $78 billion. The Texas Transportation

Institute (TTI) 2009 Urban Mobility Report (458 urban communities) estimated that drivers experienced nearly 4.2 billion hours of delay and wasted approximately 2.8 billion gallons of fuel in 2007 for a total congestion cost of $87.2 billion.

The Travel Time Index, a measure of any additional time required to make a trip during congested peak travel periods, estimated in 2008 that congested peak periods in urbanized areas required 24% more time for the same trip compared to off-peak non-congested conditions. A 30-minute trip during the off-peak time became a 37.2 minutes during the peak period. INRIX estimates that in 2018, "congestion costs each American 97 hours, or $1,348," with Boston suffering the worse congestion.

Driving on rough Texas roads costs Texas motorists a total of $5.7 billion per year in extra vehicle operating costs (VOC) such as accelerated vehicle depreciation, additional repair costs, and increased fuel consumption and tire wear. In 2014, driving on deficient roads cost each Dallas-Fort Worth-Arlington area driver a total of $1,740 per year in the form of extra VOC resulting from driving on roads in need of repair, lost time and fuel in congestion-related delays, and the cost of traffic crashes in which roadway features were a likely contributing factor (VOC= $508, congestion = $957, safety = $275). That same year, the average driver in the Dallas-Fort Worth-Arlington area lost 45 hours as a result of traffic congestion.

According to New York City transportation consultant Bruce Schaller, TNC usage in dense metropolitan areas causes significant traffic congestion. Approximately 60% of ride-hailers in these cities would have taken public transportation, walked, biked, or not made the trip if TNCs had not been available. Some 60% of ride-share customers in nine large U.S. metropolitan areas have switched from public transportation. TNCs have added 5.7 billion miles of driving annually in these metropolitan cities. Loss of service, LOS (graded A through F) could be used to estimate the percentage of congested roadways or lane miles, but not the total cost of congestion.

Both the Dallas-Fort Worth International Airport and Dallas Love Field Airport recently built new temporary parking lots to accommodate ride-hailing drivers. A significant increase in car traffic has been reported at DFW International Airport since I started ride-sharing in 2017, accompanied by increased police activity. Police control of traffic is increasing during and especially after social events, as demonstrated at the AT&T Stadium in Arlington and other venues where ride-sharing is the transportation choice for the tens of thousands of people attending events there.

DFW International Airport requires all transportation companies, including ride-hailing companies, to register and obtain a sticker for each vehicle. The airport also charges an access fee (for which TNCs transfer a standard $2 rider fee) as follows: 0-8 minutes = $4, 8-30 minutes = $2, 30 minutes to 2 hours = $3, 2-4 hours = $9, 4-6 hours = $9, 6- 24 hours = $24. The airport's entry gates often have free-flowing traffic with LOS A, but the exit gates can sometimes suffer traffic breakdowns with terrible congestion at LOS F on days like Thursday and Sunday evenings. Traffic with LOS F can also be experienced especially in Terminals C and E on days with multiple delays and cancellations due to bad weather, as well as times when multiple events take place within the Metroplex and ride-hailing drivers jam the terminals in search of their pickups.

Ride-sharing drivers are burdened with a number of seemingly minor costs that quickly add up to major expenses. Partner drivers are responsible for the running cost and maintenance of their cars. If for whatever reason a driver's car breaks down, he/she cannot rely on Uber or Lyft to repair the vehicle. Drivers are also responsible for fueling their cars and paying applicable tolls for all trip related pickups because riders are only charged for tolls incurred while they are inside the car.

Taxi drivers and chauffeurs had the 11th most dangerous job in America in 2007, with 50 fatalities, the most common of which were assaults and other violent acts. If you drive 100,000 miles (160,934.4 km) a year, which as of March 2018 is more than five times the average 18,858 miles (30,349.01 km) driven by males between the ages of 34– 54, you essentially packed more than five years of driving in just twelve months.

Despite my mastery of the Dallas-Fort Worth Metroplex cityscape, I face the inherent risk of making an error or committing a traffic violation simply because I drive so many miles in my work with Uber. There is increased risk of accidents from distraction, fatigue from prolonged driving, and optimism bias (the thinking by ride-share drivers that fatigue is more serious for "other drivers," causing them to prefer methods that are simultaneous with driving to counteract the effect of fatigue on their driving performance).

Everyone driving a vehicle today is exposed to risk, the most common of which is an accident. In 2016, collision with another motor vehicle in transport was the most common first harmful event in fatal crashes nationwide (38% of all fatal crashes). In 2017, the leading cause of severe crash or injury in Texas was from another motor vehicle in transport, accounting for 73.4%.

According to the National Highway Traffic Safety Administration (NHTSA), alcohol- impaired driving was the leading cause of car crash fatalities in 2017 (29%), followed by speeding which accounting for 26% (9,717 deaths) of all traffic fatalities that year.

Distraction-affected crashes accounted for 9% (3,166) of the 52,274 total fatalities. Texting while driving (distracted driving), driving under the influence (DUI) of your phone, just as I do when I drive under the influence of my phone (DUI-MP) during ride- sharing are therefore significant risk factors. The Uber app essentially controls and dictates all activities during trip related driving. Saturdays was the deadliest day for car crash fatalities.

Texas's overall traffic fatality rate in 2017 was 1.36 fatalities per 100 million vehicle miles of travel, higher than the national average of 1.16. Nationally, 34,247 fatal motor vehicle crashes killed 37,133 people that year. Emergency vehicles, potholes, wildlife deer), falling rocks, snowfall, torrential rains, hailstorms, tornadoes, sleet or black ice are just some of the hazards a ride-share driver can encounter while on the job.

DFW Metroplex led Texas in 2017 with the most DUI (alcohol) involved crashes and the City of Dallas ranked third after San Antonio and Houston. A 2002 LSU Department of Public Health and Preventive Medicine study ranked Dallas as the city with the most drunk driving deaths nationwide, with 10.23 deaths per 100,000 residents each year, ahead of Kansas City, Missouri (10.10 deaths) and Albuquerque (8.62 deaths).

New York Taxi Workers Alliance reports eight taxi driver suicides amid declining in- come and rising debt from the decreasing value of their medallion (the aluminum plate required to drive a cab in New York) some bought for as much as $1 million but are now only worth about $200,000 or less. Similar suicides by taxi drivers have been reported in other major cities. There is at least one reported suicide by an Uber driver in New York City.

In 2018, the New York City Council imposed a year-long cap on new licenses for ride-hailing vehicles in the city but Uber sued in February 2019 to reverse that cap. In addition to precipitating a fall in the credit of taxi drivers and the value of their medallions, ride-hailing services have worsened congestion in the city by replacing a lot of other transportation methods, such as subways, buses, bikes, and having too many drivers in circulation waiting for a ride. By leveraging an unlimited potential to recruit new ride-hailing drivers even when demand doesn't necessarily match, Uber can force market imbalances that drive down wages.

Many teenagers use ride-hailing late at night and in early morning hours while they might be coming off or going to places that I presume their parents do not know about. Hence, the safety of these adolescents and many adults is a major concern that may cost communities, as evidenced recently with the death of a 21-year old female student in Columbia, South Carolina who got into the wrong car at 2 AM mistaking it for her requested Uber ride.

Ride-share drivers spend a lot of time circulating in empty cars without passengers. In New York City from February through June 2018, almost half of the driving time was without passengers with Uber and Lyft utilization rates of 58% and 56% respectively. That rate is calculated by dividing the amount of time drivers spend on trips by the total time drivers are logged into an app (idle time plus time on a trip). If Uber riders traveled 26 billion VMT in 2018, assuming such low utilization rates, Uber drivers may have driven up to 10 billion additional miles that year just roaming the streets.

If ride-sharing removes at least one car from circulation, such low utilization rates becomes counterproductive. Uber claimed "an average wait time of five minutes for a rider to be picked up by a driver in the quarter ended December 31, 2018." The company has significantly improved its driver ETA (estimated time of arrival) to pick up a passenger at airports by use of

Rematch, in which a driver dropping a passenger is prioritized and given another ride. This makes both drivers and riders happy, due to increased productivity and earnings for the former and decreased wait time for the latter.

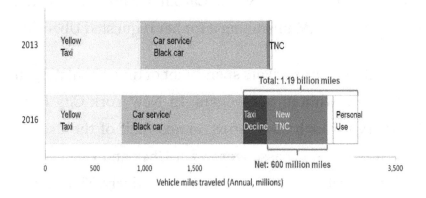

Fig. 12: Annual vehicle mileage NYC, 2013 and 2016 (Schaller Consulting). Printed with permission.

Ride-sharing adds extra VMT.

VTPI estimates that roadway expenditures not funded through vehicle user fees averaged 1-4¢ per vehicle-mile. A 2007 cost allocation study shows the road facility external costs per mile driven by automobiles/average car ($0.021), van/light truck ($0.028) and electric car ($0.051) which are the most commonly driven cars in ride-sharing. Roadway costs not borne by user charges (special fuel taxes, vehicle registration and licensing fees, road tolls and traffic fines) are all considered external costs. In 2018, Uber drivers accounted for at least $260 million to $1.04 billion in road facility external costs (calculated as (26 x 0.01) to (26 x 0.04)) given that Uber reported its consumers traveled 26 billion VMT that year alone, excluding VMT contributions from its other offerings and low utilization rates.

Before the introduction of ride-sharing companies, people relied on taxis, despite their inferior services. The only reason Uber can supply a better competing product and services at a 60% discount is that the company does not own a fleet of cars or employ any drivers. By using drivers as 1099 partners, the company avoids providing them any required employee benefits and can therefore evade such associated liabilities. Moreover, Uber does not bear any fuel, maintenance and auto insurance costs since these are transferred to the drivers. Taxis are required to carry commercial taxi insurance which may run into several hundred dollars while Uber drivers use much cheaper general liability policies. Since Uber and Lyft use their drivers as 1099 partners, each driver is essentially an independent business owner (IBO).

Drivers' 1099 tax documents from TNCs include a report on mileage traveled which I presume is data from 100% utilization rates. This reported mileage never added up to my logged odometer readings, but showed a discrepancy of 14-25%. If I traveled 88,000 miles in 2017 and Uber and Lyft logged in only 76,000, I know for sure

I did not travel 12,000 miles for my other endeavors that year. In 2018, I traveled 68,000 miles but Uber logged me in 51,000 online miles and I know for sure I did not travel 17,000 miles for my other activities.

The difference between my actual mileage traveled compared to Uber's online logs (1099 Summary) shows the extra VMT ride-share drivers travel and their low utilization rates which in my case got worse as the Dallas Market became saturated with drivers in 2018. Too many drivers have made the market competitive and kept fares low with less surges, compounded by Uber's new arithmetic surge algorithm. Such high supply of drivers is good for the customers. However, driver earnings have suffered significant declines made worse by Uber's increasing commissions.

Taxis and car rentals took a beating in 2017, based on analysis of some 50 million receipts by travel and entertainment expense management software company Certify. The report showed that Uber and Lyft accounted for 68% of overall ground transportation business expenses, with Uber having 56% of all ground transportation receipts/expenses and Lyft having 12%, while taxis accounted for 7% (down from 11% the year before) and car rentals only comprised 25%.

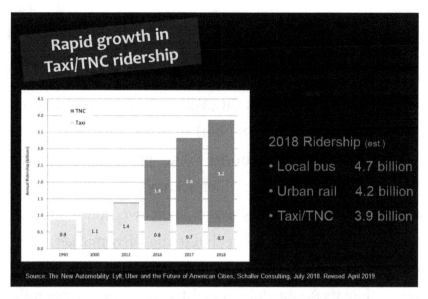

Fig. 13: TNC and taxi ridership in the U.S., 1990-2018 (Schaller Consulting). Printed with permission

There was a steady growth in taxi ridership until 2000s (about 30% increase from 2000 to 2012), reflecting growth in population, jobs and tourism in cities across the country. However, following the introduction of UberX in July 2012 for-hire ridership accelerated and TNCs have essentially crippled or stalled the taxi business in the US.

American Automobile Association, AAA estimates that in 2018, the average cost to own and operate a 2018 model vehicle was $8,849 ($0.59 per mile) for an average of 15,000 miles (24,140.16 km) traveled that year or $5,960 ($0.51 per mile) if 20,000 miles (32,186.88 km) were traveled. The average insurance cost for medium sedans was calculated at $1,232, based on the cost of fuel, maintenance, repairs, insurance, license/registration/taxes, depreciation and loan interest. Depreciation accounts for almost 40% of the cost of owning a new vehicle — more than $3,000 per year.

As of March 2018, the average American drove 13,476 miles (21687.52 km) while males in my age group (35-54 years old) drove 18,858 miles (30,349.01 km) per year. A typical New York City Yellow Taxi logged in about 70,000 miles (112,654.08 km) in 2014. In 2019, businesses can deduct up to $0.58 per mile driven for business. In its IPO filing, Uber acknowledges that in 2018, it cost on average $0.75 per mile to own and operate a vehicle in the U.S. Compare that to the DFW market at the end of 2018, when Uber charged riders $0.6/mile, which is less than its $0.64 global weighted-average cost per mile in its TAM countries as well as the $0.66 weighted-average cost per mile in its current SAM. The company also charges partners at least "25% fees on all fares," leaving drivers dependent on tax write-offs before their earnings can sustain them. The wear and tear on my car is a constant and UberX charge of $0.60 per mile driven almost matches the federal rate of $0.58 as of 2019, significantly less than the estimated $0.75/mile cost of owning and running a car in 2018 in the US. This essentially means that almost all my miles driven for Uber will be transferred to Uncle Sam when I claim such deductions. Bottom line: the federal government essentially subsidized those rides through tax savings to me.

The National Association of Insurance Commissioners' (NAI C) Auto Expenditures found that in

2016, the average expenditure for auto insurance was $935.80 ($1,008.91 in Texas). Insurance for taxi services depends on many variables, but most policies average somewhere between $5,000 and $10,000 per cab per year.

The Insurance Information Institute (III) estimates that in 2016, 77% of insured drivers purchased comprehensive coverage, as well as liability insurance, and 73% bought collision coverage. 2017 total incurred losses for insurance was $167,942,158 in 2017. The average auto liability claim for property damage was 3,638; the average auto liability claim for bodily injury was 15,270; the average collision claim was $3,425; the average comprehensive claim was $1,817. Though the number of Uber and/or Lyft drivers involved in accidents annually is unknown to the public, we do know that these companies spend much of their cost of revenue on insurance. The amount third-party insurers spend is not known as well.

In 2015, Uber cut out automakers GM, Toyota, and several intermediaries and created Xchange Leasing to lease directly to drivers but eventually shut it down in 2018.

Uber has partnered with various groups to deliver significant benefits to many communities over the years. In 2014, 50,000 military personnel earned money driving with Uber after the company launched UberMilitary. That same year, Uber riders across the U.S donated five million meals to children in need. Deaf partners have earned money driving with Uber since 2015 and Uber has partnered with Meals On Wheels America to deliver more meals to needy people since 2017.

Uber drivers earned over $78.2 billion from 2015 to 2018, and received $1.2 billion in tips since July 2017 when in-app tipping was launched. Lyft's IPO filing claimed $10 billion of driver earnings since inception, and the company's latest update on lifetime driver tips amounts to $500 million. Uber offers Employee Resource Groups (ERGs) to its employees, while Lyft actually has a Driver Advisory Council specifically dedicated to driver relations.

Lyft claimed its riders helped stimulate local spending by more than $2.5 billion in 2018, while Uber claimed its platform supported $17.0 billion in annualized gross domestic product in the U.S. through income generated directly and indirectly by its drivers, based on data collected between June and August 2017. Its Round Up & Donate program has enabled riders to donate over $10 million in 20 million rides to partner charities since May 2017 for a range of causes (supporting military service members, combatting homelessness and fighting cancer). Lyft also expects to invest the greater of 1% of its profits or $50 million annually toward certain social impact efforts.

Uber's IPO filing awarded "appreciation awards" to drivers in "good standing" with at least one trip in 2019 prior to April 7, 2019. The following amounts were given for the corresponding lifetime trips: $100 for 2,500 trips, $500 for 5K trips, $1K for 10K trips, and $10K for 20K trips. Regrettably, I only received $100 for my 4,791 trips since trip counting was unfairly not prorated. Lyft only awarded $1K for 10K trips, and $10K for 20K trips in its IPO filing.

CHAPTER 7

TNC LIABILITIES AND UBER'S BAD BEHAVIORS

Uber is the fastest growing startup company in the history of innovation. The explosive expansion of TNCs in fewer than 10 years and the disruptions in the taxi sector resulted in some significant fast-moving events. Notable among them was a cascade of negative media attention between late 2016 and early 2017 that almost brought Uber down. This turbulent period, especially 2017, was a culmination of a history of very bad behaviors, arrogance, intimidations, spying, tech terrorism and stretching to the bounds of that which is tolerable, and many times even breaking the law. Stories of assaults, sexual exploitation and misconducts, privacy violations and driver partner exploitation and disrespect dominated national news during that period.

The pinnacle of Uber's 2017 meltdown followed a January 30th revolt on its surge pricing at JFK International Airport in New York City early that year which triggered the "#deleteUber" movement on Twitter that cost the company substantial user defections and benefited rival Lyft, which saw an almost 60% rise in new

104

user subscriptions. Its then CEO and cofounder Travis Kalanick was an open supporter of newly-elected President Donald Trump and his choice to join Trump's advisory council infuriated many of the company's liberal users and its significant immigrant driver population. In January 2017, Lyft surpassed Uber in iOS downloads for the first time and Uber's U.S. market share has since dropped from more than 80% down to about 70% or less.

As a result, Uber, which had started off as a brilliant team of engineers and entrepreneurs, needed to transition into a corporation with new management. Dara Khosrowshahi, the former Expedia CEO who is acknowledged as a master of dynamic pricing, was brought in to replace Mr. Kalanick.

Uber hired former U.S. Attorney General Eric Holder (Covington & Burling LLP) to review its workplace culture and practices. The company's Board of Directors in June 2017 accepted the recommendations in Mr. Holder's report and Uber launched the "180 Days of Change" campaign targeted at improving the company's work environment and relationships with its drivers. As one of those drivers, I experienced the implementation of all the different phases of this campaign, which in my opinion were necessary and significantly improved driver relations. In-app tipping was added, as was the two-minute cancellation time.

Uber's earnings structure changed. Drivers were offered injury protection they could obtain for a fee, a 24/7 driver phone support line was introduced, and $15 fee for lost items was implemented. Drivers received notification for long and short rides, as well as trips previously scheduled by riders, including compensation for long pickups. Lyft already had some of these features when I started driving for that company in early 2017. The campaign also introduced a live rider location system and balanced the rating system. The end result: Uber's corporate behaviors were eventually forced to change due to rider, driver, investor and public pressure.

Uber reported in its IPO filing that it has liable costs "associated with defending, settling, or resolving pending and future lawsuits (including demands for arbitration) relating to the independent contractor status of drivers." In March 2019, it reached a preliminary $20 million settlement (subject to a final approval hearing in July 2019) in two class action lawsuits filed by drivers who contracted with the company in California and Massachusetts:

1. O'Connor, et al., v. Uber Technologies, Inc. and
2. Yucesoy v. Uber Technologies, Inc., et al.

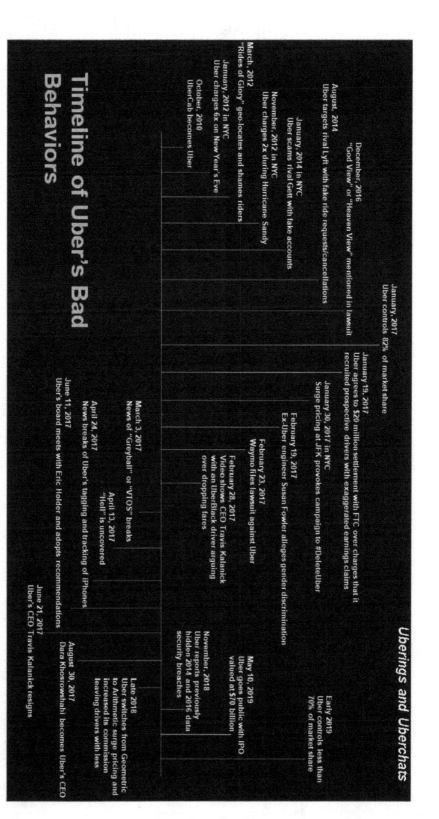

Fig. 14: Uber's long history of opportunistic and very bad behaviors

In its IPO filing, Uber also reports that more than 60,000 of its drivers who had entered into arbitration agreements filed (or expressed an intention to file) arbitration demands against the company asserting similar claims as above.

The company suffered similar changes in Europe during 2017 for its status as a technology company, where its TNC intermediation service was declassified from an "'information society service' to a 'service in the field of transport'." Uber's services the Court of Justice in the European Union argued in May 2017, "amounts to the organization and management of a comprehensive system for on-demand urban transport." This forced the company in different EU jurisdictions to abide by local labor and other requirements.

Uber subsidiary Exchange Leasing approved me for a car in early 2017 but I declined because I believe that leasing a car for ride-hailing is a bad idea. Desperate individuals with few alternatives easily become entrapped in exorbitant weekly payment requirements, which an unseasoned ride-sharing driver will likely find hard to meet. One DFW area Uber driver complained in late 2017 that Uber leased him a 2016 Chevy Cruise for $146 a week, which is about $7,592 a year for a car worth less than $12,000, according to Carfax. The car had mechanical issues needing repair work that would cost more than

$1000. In 2017, Uber was reported to have knowingly rented fire-prone cars on recall for serious safety concerns to its drivers in Singapore.

In January 2017, Uber was fined $20 million by the Federal Trade Commission (FTC) for its Vehicle Solutions Program's misleading earnings claims that "Uber Drivers can earn specific high hourly and yearly earnings." The company "exaggerated earning claims and claims about financing through its vehicle solutions program." The FTC found that "in many instances, drivers have not earned the high earnings touted by Uber." How much an Uber driver or the average ride-sharing driver actually makes is an ongoing debate, yet these companies still decline to grant access to such related data for public analysis.

Lyft had several similar class action lawsuits for driver classification on its platform as independent contractors. The company reported settling one in September 2013 for $27 million and another in 2018 for $1.95 million. In its IPO filing, Lyft reported contracts with insurance providers that require "reinsurance premiums to be deposited into restricted trust accounts with a third-party financial institution, from which the insurance providers are reimbursed for claim payments" and the company tucked away $863.7 million at the end of 2018 vs. $360.9 million in 2017. Uber reserved $2.94 billion at the end of 2018 vs. $2.0 billion at the end of 2017.

While Uber was facing these challenges at the corporate level, end-user level ride- sharing driver related issues garnered negative media coverage. The most reputation-damaging case involved a 48-year-old Michigan Uber driver named Jason Dalton, who murdered six people in a February 2016 shooting rampage. He blamed his actions on the Uber app that he claimed turned him into a "puppet" and helped him pick his victims, since some of the deaths occurred between rides.

Uber made a reported $1 million pre-suit settlement with a pedestrian incapacitated after being hit by one of its drivers in Miami. Other drivers for both Lyft and Uber have been accused of sexually assaulting their passenger, including on Arevalos-Avalos, a citizen of El Salvador in the U.S. illegally, yet successfully driving for Uber. In 2018, CNN uncovered 103 Uber drivers accused of crimes or named in a civil lawsuit.

Uber and Lyft drivers have had near misses, been challenged, abused or assaulted by passengers with nefarious intents or compromised behaviors from riders with severe alcohol intoxication or substance abuse. The most consequential of these is that of Former Uber CEO Travis Kalanick in an UberBlack disrespectfully challenging the driver regarding fares. Other videos show drivers being beaten, their cars stolen and engaging in arguments. One driver was stabbed to death in the Bronx borough of New York City.

Other challenges for the company involved an intellectual property theft lawsuit from Google's parent company, Alphabet, pertaining to Waymo's self-driving car technology. In February 2017, Waymo sued Uber for theft of trade secrets and patent infringement by Ottomotto LLC co-founder Anthony Levandowski for downloading "14,000 highly confidential" files to an external hard drive, including the design for the company's LiDAR circuit board when he left Google's moonshot labs. In February 2018, Uber entered a settlement agreement with Waymo to not misappropriate Waymo intellectual property.

The U.S. Department of Justice and the Portland Bureau of Transportation (PBOT) all investigated Uber's "Greyball" or Violation of Terms of Services ("VTOS") project the company used to circumvent the law or evade authorities—identify, spy on and deny services to certain riders—first revealed in December 2014 in Portland, OR. Uber typically uses a "standard" view on riders' phone when they try to request a ride. However, they have the ability for marketing, functionality, safety of driver-partners, and for some bad behaviors when caught. The company gives the following examples for hiding the standard view:

1. showing cars that bear the logo of the successful team in their local market
2. displaying a new functionality being testing to a test group of employees
3. hiding from individuals determined to pose a threat to driver-partners

I referenced my "Batman Car" view in Chapter 3. A rider brought it to my attention and after learning of "Greyball" I understood what it looks like. I confess that it was a fascinating and captivating view that made me look like a comic book superhero. But what did that really mean? Is Uber categorizing its drivers who speed, drive a lot, are effective or efficient? Are they categorizing passengers who are always in a hurry and those who exhibit bad behaviors? What are their metrics and threshold? How are these end-users micro-targeted and for what benefit to whom? Uber knows even more but I may never be able to figure out why they made me a star to my rider that day and how many other times they may have greyballed me without my knowledge. One possible reason (as Uber explained above) could have been in support of the Dallas Cowboys, which had a local game against the Tennessee Titans the day this happened.

Another covert Uber program is the "God View" tool that allowed employees to access and track rider and customer locations without their knowledge or permission.

Uber was fined $20,000 by federal regulators after one of its executives tracked a New York BuzzFeed News reporter in 2014.

Uber's "Hell" program used public domain data to spy on its rival Lyft back in 2017, or even before. "Hell" tracked Lyft drivers by creating fake Lyft customer accounts that Uber then used to trick Lyft's app's system into finding. Through such spying activity on cross-dispatching or drivers that drove on both Uber and Lyft platforms, Uber can then match or beat its rival's price offerings and driver incentives.

Talking about spying on others, how about shaming your customers publicly. According to the Intelligencer, Uber once shared a blog post of its rider data that analyze customers taking "Rides of Glory," for rides requested from 10 p.m. to 4 a.m. on Fridays and Saturdays, followed by a second ride requested by the same rider hours later from the same place they were dropped off earlier in the evening. Such awkward on-demand shaming of their customers, to no fault of the latter, shows the arrogant attitude Uber started off with back in 2012.

Uber has faced many other challenges, some international, and has been sued, restricted or outright banned from certain markets. The company was sued by a

26-year-old Indian woman whose Uber driver brutally raped her in New Delhi in December 2014.

An Uber executive illegally obtained the woman's medical records after the incident without her consent.

Such corporate irresponsibility contributed to the suspension of Uber's 2017 application for a new license to operate in London by Transport for London, where 3.5 million riders and more than 40,000 licensed drivers rely on the company to make a living. In June 2018, the company was awarded a 15-month short-term license to operate in London again. That same year, the company suspended its services in Barcelona, Spain again after the city imposed a 15-minute delay before passenger pickup following taxi driver protests. This follows its re-entry in 2016 into that market with UberX, which uses fully licensed ride-hailing services that meet local transportation laws, as opposed to its previous UberPop offering that was expelled from the city in late 2014. These are just a few of the challenges that Uber faces in many cities and localities around the world, as some communities try to protect their local taxi industries.

Even in its corporate structure, Uber was besieged under the carefree leadership of Travis Kalanick by claims of sexism and sexual harassment, and workplace violations.

Uber often exploits its status as a tech company and its versatile innovative ability to operate at the edge of the law, rather than develop a sustainable business model that will stand the test of time.

Under the leadership of its new CEO Dara Khosrowshahi the company revealed in November 2017, the occurrence of a May 2014 and a Fall 2016 security and data privacy breach. In the 2014 breach, an outside actor had gained access to 100,000 drivers' personal information (names, driver's license numbers, bank accounts and domestic routing numbers, and social security numbers) after an Uber employee with "God View" access unintentionally posted it publicly.

In October and November of 2016, outside actors targeted both drivers and consumers and got away with personal data of about 57 million people worldwide (names, email addresses, mobile phone numbers, and drivers' license numbers of approximately 600,000 drivers). Uber, instead of reporting the stolen data as required by law in this 2016 breach, paid the hackers a ransom of $100,000 under former CEO Travis Kalanick and referred to the payment as "bug bounty," NPR reported. Uber ultimately settled for $148 million in September 2018 with the Attorneys General from all 50 states and the District of Columbia who had joined the suit, one year into new CEO Dara Khosrowshahi's term.

The ascension of Dara Khosrowshahi to the helm marked a new direction for Uber. Amid negative media attention, a demoralized workforce, poor organizational culture and driver offenses, many structural changes were implemented and apologies issued. The company embarked on a massive media blitz estimated to reach $500 million and nearly doubled its marketing spending in 2018 over 2016 spending. I remember seeing a television interview with Mr. Khosrowshahi in which he talked about his Iranian upbringing and how those values will implicitly shape his leadership and direction for Uber. While his near-term objective as set by Uber's Board of Directors is to take the company public in 2019, Uber must begin to reckon with labor relations changes already taking grip in Europe where courts are ruling that the company must treat its drivers as employees.

CHAPTER 8

IPO: HOW MUCH IS IT REALLY WORTH?

Uber aims to help Americans save on the more than $1 trillion they spend every year owning and operating their cars, which they only use 5% of the time. The global sharing economy generated some $18.6 billion in 2017 and the Americas are expected to account for more than half of the sharing economy market's total revenue, which Goldman Sachs projects at $285 billion by 2030. As of May 2018, Uber was the leading ride-hailing operator worldwide and in the United States, with a market value between $68 and $76 billion, followed by China's Didi Chuxing at between $50 and $56 billion. In early December 2018, it was reported that both Uber and Lyft secretly filed for IPOs to go public sometime in the first half of 2019. Uber used Morgan Stanley and Goldman Sachs while Lyft picked JP Morgan Chase. Lyft, initially valued at about $15 billion opened its IPO valued at $22.2 billion at the end of its first day of trading on March 29, 2019. Lyft had lost almost a quarter of its market cap at the time of this publication. Uber, with a pre-IPO value of about $76 billion opened its IPO with a dismal $70 billion valuation at the end of its first day of trading on May 10, 2019.

High-income urban dwellers are more than twice as likely to use ride-hailing services, compared to high-income people living in rural areas—71 % compared to 32%. Seventy percent of Uber and Lyft trips occur in nine large U.S. metropolitan areas and in eight of these (except New York City) they account for 90% of taxi rides (in Boston, Chicago, Los Angeles, Miami, New York, Philadelphia, San Francisco, Seattle and Washington DC metro areas). According to ABI Research, 16 billion ride-hailing trips were completed globally in 2017 with 70% of them taking place in Asia, while another 24 billion trips were expected to be completed in 2018. An Uber sponsored ERG study found that most people used Uber for leisure, compared to using their own cars more for personal use. Lyft reported in its IPO filing that almost half (47%) of its rides occurred during winter.

In May 2018, 76% of U.S. survey respondents were familiar with Uber's ride-sharing services. Thirty-six percent of U.S. adults said in 2018 that they have used a ride-hailing service such as Uber or Lyft, doubling the 15% reported in 2015 according to Pew Research. Both men and women use Uber equally. An independent study of Uber billing emails found that the median number of rides taken by all riders in the first two weeks is two, and users who had more than two rides in their first two weeks tend to continue to use the services. A majority of men become active but older users, users with more expensive rides, users of more expensive car types (such as UberBlack), and users with a higher fraction of their rides on weekends, have been shown to be less likely to become active Uber riders.

Most TNC trips do not replace personal auto trips; instead, they mostly replace transit, walking and biking trips, thus creating entirely new miles on city streets. An Uber commissioned study by Economic Development Research Group (EDR) that compared data from U.S. Department of Transportation's National Household Travel Survey, NHTS to data from Uber users found that most trips Uber riders make are for leisure but when people use their personal cars, they mostly make personal trips.

Schaller Consulting estimates that about 20% of TNC users in major U.S. cities would have used a personal vehicle if the TNC were not available, and 20% would have taken a taxicab. People without a vehicle use TNC at a higher rate than those who have one.

Schaller Consulting estimates that about 20% of TNC users in major U.S. cities would have used a personal vehicle if the TNC were not available, and 20% would have taken a taxicab. People without a vehicle use TNC at a higher rate than those who have one.

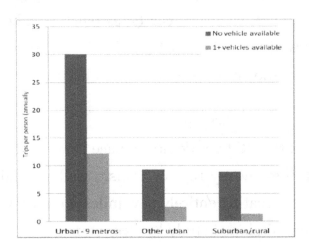

Fig. 15: TNC trip rates by whether vehicle is available to the household. (Schaller Consulting). Printed with permission

Uber clearly dominates the worldwide ride-share industry. It operates in 700 cities with its Personal Mobility offering in 63 countries and about 70% of U.S. ride-share spending in 2018, 91 million MAPCs (Monthly Active Platform Consumers), 3.9 million drivers (worldwide), $78 billion lifetime driver earnings, 10 billion lifetime rides, 26 billion VMT in 2018 alone, more than15 million rides per day and 155 million downloads of its app (19.6% from Brazil and 17.1% from the US) in 2018. Uber makes 250 million trips either to or from airports every year, representing about 5% of the departures and arrivals at airports around the world. In 2018, Uber lost $3.3 billion, excluding gains from the sale of its overseas business units in Russia and Southeast Asia. Net earnings was $1.0 billion in 2018 propelled by sale of those foreign interests compared to a 2017 net loss of $4.0 billion.

According to Barney Harford, Uber's Chief Operating Officer (COO), as of September 2017 Uber for Business had 65,000 organizations around the world using Uber for Business to procure transportation services for their employees and their customers. UberEats, the company's food delivery service started in 2015 currently serves 15 million UberEats users and 220,000 UberEats restaurants in 500 cities across 35 countries. UberEats revenue grew from $103 million in 2016 to $1.5 billion at the end of 2018. Uber's corporate labor force grew from 159 employees in 2013 to 22,263 global employees in 2018, half of whom are located outside the United States. There are 500 Uber Greenlight Hubs (offices) worldwide.

Uber Freight for shippers launched in the US in May 2017 and has contracts with more than 36,000 carriers that in aggregate employ more than 400,000 drivers and have served in excess of 1,000 shippers, including more than 100 enterprise shippers and global enterprises such as Anheuser-Busch InBev, Niagara, Land O'Lakes, and Colgate- Palmolive. In 2018, Uber Freight's revenue grew to more than $125 million, with 12% of U.S. truckers using the service. Uber Freight is already in the EU truckload market, the third globally after China with an estimated worth of $400 billion and is considered to be inefficiently operated Uber's IPO filing showed its dockless e-bikes and e-scooters are available in 12 cities as of December 31, 2018, and the Dallas market is certainly one of them with the e-scooters almost omnipresent in Downtown areas.

In its IPO filing, the company reported direct partnerships with global chains like McDonald's, Subway, Popeyes, and local restaurants that can sign up to work with UberEats on a self-service basis. Uber enables them to offer in-app direct marketing to consumers with personalized, sponsored advertisements. Its acquisition of orderTalk facilitates the ordering process by using stored consumer order history and payment information to integrate directly with many restaurants' point-of-sale systems to help them analyze orders and predict demand.

Uber's hassle-free technologies include Instant Cash for drivers to cash out immediately and Uber Cash for customers to add funds or save credit cards. The company has also partnered with AXA in Europe to "provide drivers with access to a range of additional accident, injury, illness, and maternity and paternity benefits" as well as CarAdvise in the U.S. for "discounted vehicle maintenance and servicing."

Uber joint ventures and partners include Yandex.Taxi, and OEMs such as Toyota, Volvo, and Daimler for its autonomous vehicle. The company also launched Uber Health in March 2018 to transport patients.

Lyft in its IPO filing claimed 18.6 million active riders, 1.4 million drivers, one billion lifetime rides, more than one million rides per day, 76 million lifetime airport trips, and a 39% market share in 2018. There are some 65 million Lyft App installs. The company operates in nearly 300 cities, employing 4,791 people in some fifty offices and Driver Hubs. Its revenue grew from $200 million in 2015 to $2.16 billion in 2018, with a revenue per active rider of $36.04. The company has 95% US coverage plus Canada as only international market, and claims 52% of its riders use Lyft to commute to work. Contrast that usage to Uber's majority use for leisure trips (Fig. 15). Lyft reports multiplier effect from existing riders booking more rides year-over-year, 35% more riders in 2018 with 65% more rides and a 75% increase in the total value of rides. The average Lyft fare is $13 from which it lost $1.56 ($3.50 commission but $5.06 operating cost) in 2018, down from $4.30 per ride in 2016 when the company spent most of its revenue on sales and marketing. Lyft's spending on sales and promotions dropped from $2.60 per ride in 2016 to $1.30 per ride in 2018.

The following series of charts and tables roughly compare Uber and Lyft, trending a big picture of their growth, revenue, expenses and loses since 2016 based on their IPO filings. The data and charts depict Uber's scale compared to Lyft but also appreciate the latter's growth.

Fig 16: Comparison of active users on both Uber and Lyft platforms. Uber reports Monthly Active Platform Consumers, MAPC. Lyft reports only quarterly tally of active riders. (Data from Uber and Lyft S-1, SEC and Stanford/Uber, 2019)

Monthly Active Platform Consumers/Active Users (millions)			
Year		Lyft	Uber
2016	Annual		45
	Q1	3.5	
	Q2	4.5	
	Q3	5.7	
	Q4	6.6	
2017	Annual		68
	Q1	8.1	
	Q2	9.4	
	Q3	11.4	
	Q4	12.6	
2018	Annual		91
	Q1	14	
	Q2	15.5	
	Q3	17.4	
	Q4	18.6	

a)

Basic summary statistics, all US Uber drivers (UberX/UberPOOL driver-weeks in the US from January 2015 - March 2017)			
	All	Men	Women
Weekly earnings	$376.38	$397.68	$268.18
Hourly earnings	$21.07	$21.28	$20.04
Hours per week	17.06	17.98	12.82
Trips per week	29.83	31.52	21.83
6 month attrition rate	68.10%	65.00%	76.50%
Number of drivers	1,873,474	1,361,289	512,185
Number driver/weeks	24,832,168	20,210,399	4,621,760
Number of Uber trips7	740,627,707	646,965,269	93,662,438

b)

Fig 17: Lyft reported 1 billion (1186.4) rides compared to Uber's10 billion (10774). Rough 2017 reflected in Uber's growth in ridership marked by inflexion in the line chart. (Data from Uber and Lyft S-1, SEC)

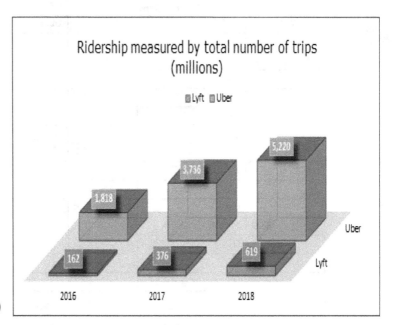

a)

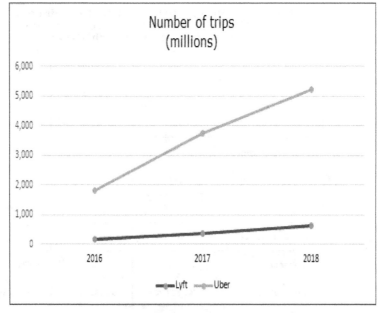

b)

Fig. 18: Lyft has been doubling its bookings. Uber continues to grow, albeit much slower and is still more valuable. Lyft bookings grew 140.8% between 2016 and 2017, but only expanded 75.6% between 2017 and 2018. Some variations in how both companies reported this revenue. (Data from Uber and Lyft S-1, SEC)

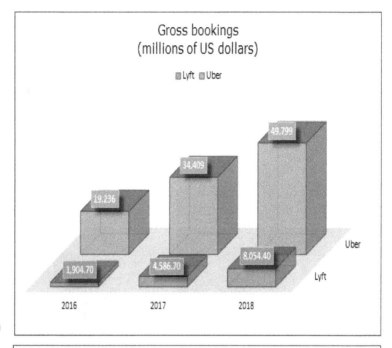

a)

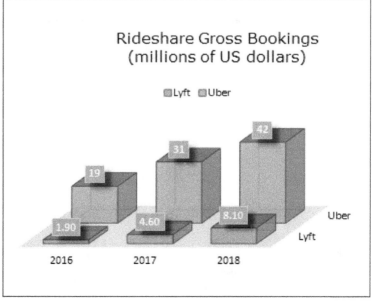

b)

Fig. 19: Uber generates more revenue than Lyft, but has lost significant ground to Lyft. Lyft's revenue grew 209% between 2016 and 2017, followed by an impressive but slower 103% between 2017 and 2018. Its revenue as a percentage of bookings grew from 16.8% in 2016-Q1 to 28.7% in 2018-Q4. (Data from Uber and Lyft S-1, SEC)

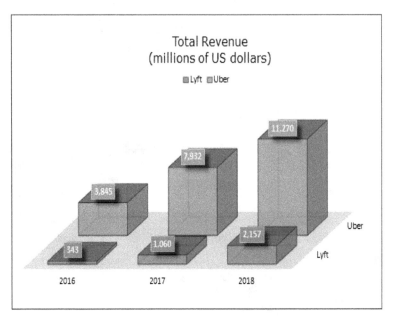

a)

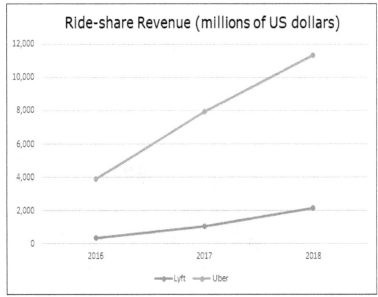

b)

Fig. 20: Both Uber and Lyft are just very expensive to run. They burn cash to spur their meteoric rise. (Data from Uber and Lyft S-1, SEC)

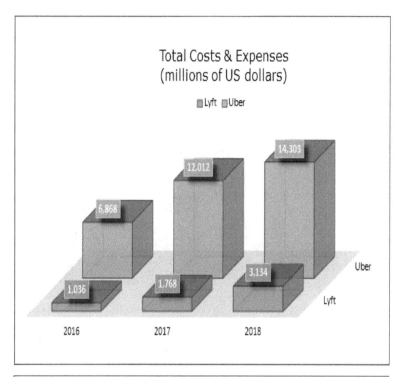

a)

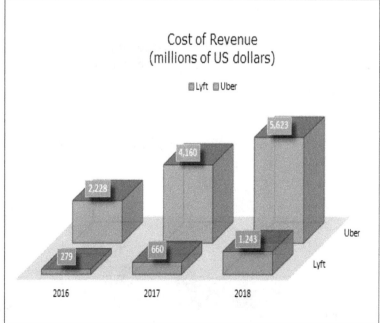

b)

Fig. 21: Both Uber and Lyft are hemorrhaging cash. In 2018, Uber sold some of its overseas interests in Asia. (Data from Uber and Lyft S-1, SEC)

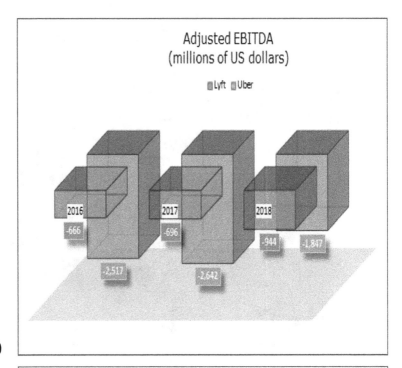

a)

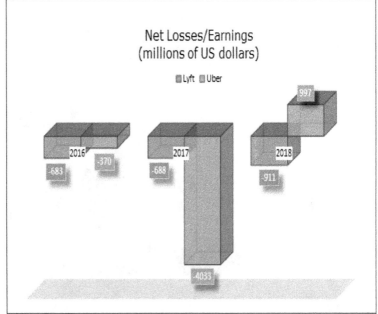

b)

Fig. 22: After paying for the cost of doing business, Uber and Lyft are essentially marketing companies.

Uber still invests significantly in Research and Development and as a driver partner, I can attest to their superiority and scalability as well as customizability. Such huge investments in R&D by Uber found boundless intriguing possibilities, some of which were abused. (Data from Uber and Lyft S-1, SEC)

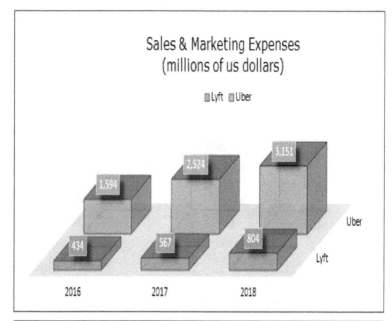

a)

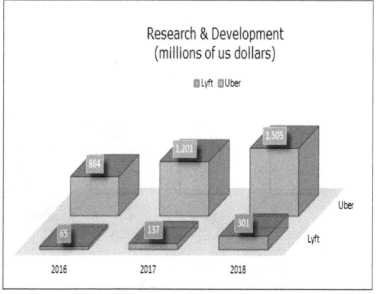

b)

Fig. 23: Uber and Lyft are expensive to operate despite their lean technologies because of the risks involved in their short-term business model. (Data from Uber and Lyft S-1, SEC)

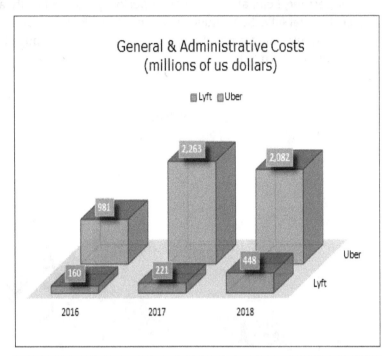

a)

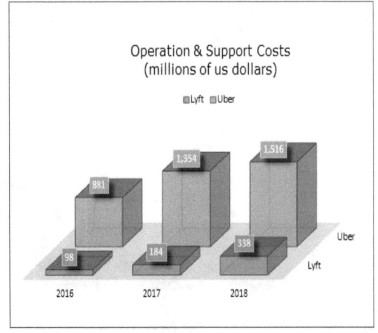

b)

Fig. 24: Lyft essentially marketed itself to prominence, especially following Uber's challenges. Lyft still doesn't have control over its costs and expenses. Uber has better control over its costs and expenses than Lyft does. (Data from Uber and Lyft S-1, SEC)

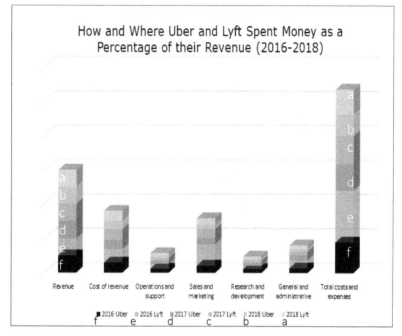

a)

b)

Fig. 25: Growth in Uber is clearly slowing. (Data from Uber and Lyft S-1, SEC)

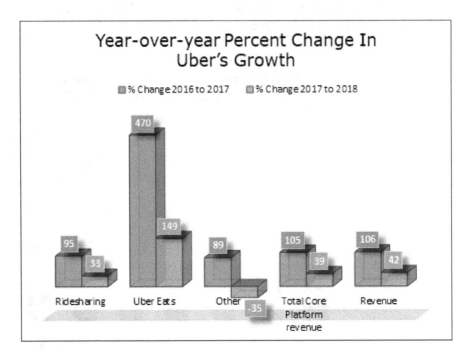

Uber defines a long-term total addressable market ("TAM"), and a currently serviceable addressable market ("SAM"). Its Personal Mobility TAM consists of 11.9 trillion miles per year or 19.15 trillion kilometers (7.5 trillion passenger vehicle miles [12.07 trillion kilometers] and 4.4 trillion public transportation miles [7.08 trillion kilometers]) traveled in 175 countries with an estimated $5.7 trillion market opportunity ($4.7 trillion from passenger vehicles and $1 trillion from public transportation). Its current Personal Mobility SAM has 57 countries with 5.8 trillion vehicle miles (9.33 trillion kilometers), plus six other countries making up its near-term priorities. That represents an additional 1.2 trillion vehicle miles (1.93 trillion kilometers), resulting in 7.0 trillion total vehicle miles (11.27 trillion kilometers).

Uber estimates that 68% of passenger vehicle miles are driven on trips of fewer than 30 miles (48.28 km) representing 3.9 trillion vehicle miles (6.28 trillion kilometers) of its current SAM and a $3.0 trillion near-term SAM. The company uses the average cost of operating an automobile in the U.S. and Canada (equal purchasing power parity, PPP), $0.75 for both its TAM and SAM to calculate other rates in different countries with a PPP multiplier. From these estimates, the company then applies the 91 million MAPCs on its platform to obtain a penetration rate of 2% of the 4.1 billion people who reside in its 63 near-term SAM countries. Uber also believes that in the 63 near-term SAM countries,

4.1 billion people in 2017 traveled 4.7 trillion vehicle miles (7.56 trillion kilometers) in trips fewer than 30 miles (48.28 km). Of that number, 16.5 billion miles (26.55 billion kilometers) were traveled on its platform, representing less than a 0.5% penetration. The following year, the company reports a stagnant 4.1 billion people in those same countries traveled the same 4.7 trillion vehicle miles (26.55 billion kilometers) in trips fewer than 30 miles (48.28 km), of which 26 billion miles (41.84 billion kilometers) were traveled on its platform. That still represents less than 1% penetration.

Uber focused its TAM and SAM analysis for distances less than 3 miles (4.83 km), between three miles (4.83 km) to 30 miles (48.28 km), and greater than 30 miles (48.28 km).

Using similar logic, its SAM for UberEats is worth $795 billion of the $2.8 trillion consumer food service industry in 2017 (including $2.0 trillion eat-in restaurant spending and $161 billion in home delivery spending), of which its penetration rate of 1% was based on $7.9 billion of UberEats gross bookings for the year ended December 31, 2018. The company sees opportunities in retail, given the $6.3 trillion store-based grocery retail spending made in 2017.

A similar analysis also gives the company a less than 0.1% penetration of the $700 billion serviceable freight market, given its $359 million of Uber Freight gross bookings for the year ended December 31, 2018.

Major financing and ownership histories of Uber and Lyft include:

- Uber as of October 2018 had organized 22 funding rounds and raised a total of $24.2 billion with its biggest investor being Softbank Vision Fund
- Lyft as of June 2018 had organized 18 funding rounds and raised a total of $5.1 billion with its biggest investor being CapitalG

Uber's deficit totaled $7.9 billion as of December 31, 2018. Since 2010, the company has raised funds through equity and debt financings for its operations. A significant portion of those funds were used to discount fares by so much that in 2015, Uber passengers were paying only 41% of the actual cost of their trips, and the company doled out bonuses to drivers that have at times exceeded $1,000. As Uber continues to bleed billions in loses, these subsidies must eventually be phased out and the fear is that such price rate increase to its consumers may lead to decrease ride volumes. Historically, when taxis raised fares by 20%, they lost 4% to 5% of their customers and Uber may not be immune to similar consequences. The company already experiences a drop in ridership with any price surges.

Lyft's cash burn rate in 2018 was $600 million; at such rate, it will run out of money in four years. At nearly $2.2 billion in revenue in 2018, Lyft's IPO market cap of $22.2 billion on March 29 gave the company a price-to-sales ratio of 10.1. Since historically high growth tech companies see their IPO multiple compress by 10% per year, if Lyft can keep its revenue growing faster than 10%, its stock price will keep increasing even without profitability. Lyft's cost of revenue, worsened by its insurance liabilities, offers a bleak picture of the company's ability to achieve profitability. If it continues to grow at 70% a year, twice the rate of rival Uber, without any added cost of revenue, it may break even in 2021. The company's corporate costs are currently $3.00 per ride while rider growth in 2018 was 11%. Failure of companies like SNAP, which is worth less than half its IPO after two years demonstrates that Lyft can be exposed to similar risk of failure from factors like regulations, litigations, or an Uber resurgence.

Uber, on the other hand, has implemented significant structural changes at the corporate, customer and driver levels, and for the most part its CEO Dara Khosrowshahi has stabilized the ship and seems to be steering it in a new direction. That direction is still going to be challenging given the company's treatment of drivers in regard to earnings.

Uber expects $10 to $11 billion in net revenue during 2019 without profitability for the next three years, and its IPO on May 10, 2019, valued the company at $70 billion, at a 6.2x the price-to-sales basis (2018 sales). Nearly 80% of ride-share drivers work for at least two platforms, and 60% of those drive mostly for Uber, compared to 17% for Lyft. Seventy- six percent of Lyft drivers expressed satisfaction with their driving experience, compared to only 58% for Uber.

Since more drivers are satisfied driving for Lyft and, like me, they end up driving more for Uber due to its market share, Lyft does have the opportunity to tap into this satisfaction gap if Uber stumbles again. However, given Uber's proven ability to scale, a stable management and good driver and customer outreach may again be detrimental to Lyft. Although Lyft pioneered the ride-share industry, Uber came from behind and dominated it.

Uber Pro is an Uber Partner Rewards program in which partners must complete a certain number of rides per month to become eligible for gas discounts. Lyft uses this system for drivers to qualify for subsidized rental car payments and in December 2018, it launched Lyft Rewards, a loyalty program for riders to encourage repeat use. In late 2018, Uber launched a new rewards program called Uber Rewards for customers, offering such benefits as premium support, complimentary upgrades, best-rated drivers and priority pickups, price protection and free cancellation gained through points from rides and UberEats. Rewards levels are Blue, Gold, Platinum and Diamond and follow the same principles as used in credit card and airline travel rewards.

My last UberSelect rider in February 2019 told me he was automatically enrolled in the program. These rewards and their associated benefits should help Uber build customer following but customer loyalty must be earned from consistently treating them uniquely and customizing products and services to make them happy.

Uber's challenges as it goes public are both financial and technological; public scrutiny and audits may reveal certain unsustainable practices. The company needs proper management and strategy and a comprehensive plan for its drivers. I believe there was a missed opportunity to incorporate driver interests in changes the company undertook in preparation for its IPO.

Uber controls more than twice the market share than Lyft, generates five times more revenue, spends five times on R&D, is valued at more than four times the size of Lyft, and continues to grow, albeit slower than Lyft.

Based on my field experience and analysis, Lyft has been taking the nice, friendly, fix- everything-wrong-with-Uber approach since I first joined them in 2017. Amidst Uber's meltdown, Lyft doubled down on a lot of things they were already doing right and also benefited from being the only known alternative in the US with broad coverage. That strategy has continued to pay off as Lyft continues to grow faster than Uber, though both companies are growing much slower than their exponential rise between 2012 and 2018.

Uber on the other hand has implemented significant structural changes both at the corporate, customer and driver levels and for the most part, its CEO Dara Khosrowshahi has stabilized the ship and seems to be steering it in a new direction. That direction is still going to be challenging given the company's treatment of drivers with regards to earnings.

Uber is a master at scalability and though I believe they can resurge, both Lyft and Uber have some challenging times ahead given how bad they continue to treat their drivers even as they go public.

Uber must continue to improve on its service reliability, the consistency of its driver supply and price stability. It must also focus on maintainability, the sleek and efficient hassle-free simplicity of its app and functional background processes involved in trip fulfillment. These metrics and other key performance indicators should be measured and continually improved upon to ensure that Uber's products and services are dependable. Such dependability will only be achieved with proper treatment of one of its major stakeholders, the partner drivers.

Uber may be years away from profitability, but given the company's proven experience on scaling operations, it can find ways to cut cost of operations and reduce its liabilities. It must continue to improve on its corporate governance to ensure stability and better relations with its customers. Cooperative dealings with its drivers will be key to building or bridging those relationships so Uber must start working on different scenarios and models to best accommodate its drivers as employees or quasi-employees, combining better pay and some minimum guaranteed benefits.

As I've pointed out, Uber has access to our media and data through our phones. It sells us food, transports us and therefore stands to benefit significantly from continually engineering our behaviors through manipulations of such data to increase its market value for its investors while continuing to innovate in order to help us more efficiently navigate and enjoy our daily lives. Will Uber and Lyft start selling our data like Facebook and Google have? Maybe they already do, and we just don't know it.

The week after Uber's dismal yet gigantic IPO of $70 billion in market cap, the company sent out personalized driver stats in a video compilation and encourage its driver partners like me to share with their riders. It was a beautifully done piece of work and all my riders who watched it were impressed. I already know Uber keeps those statistics about me, and I was not surprised with the video compilation. I know they also know a lot more about my non-Uber related activities and may be cashing in on them as well as on yours too.

The video shows that I have driven for Uber for over two years, shared more than 4700 trips with riders from 43 countries. Fifteen percent of those trips were at dawn (mostly airport trips I'm sure) while 11% were at sunset. I definitely earned the $100 bonus Uber gave me on its way to its IPO!

On the other hand, the platform does offer significant opportunities for economics, social, behavioral and clinical studies. The opportunities for marketing on these platforms are many and will have to be done right. There is room for front-end advertisements, sales, dating (one rider suggested), and healthcare/mobile clinic (some vitals). I believe Uber already monetizes the back-end, but to what extent? Only Uber insiders may know.

CHAPTER 9

THE FUTURE OF MOBILITY

To better assess and compare the different modes of transportation, mobility, defined as "the movement of people and goods, measured in terms of travel distance and speed" and measured as person-miles or person-trips makes for a better standard. Lyft blames premature deaths from pollution (58,050 in 2005 alone) on people being trapped in an expensive, unhealthy and inefficient car ownership ecosystem, further claiming that humans need not own cars to enjoy their benefits. The company envisions a full shift from personal vehicles to a service-based Transportation-as-a-Service (TaaS) subscription model that offers safer, more affordable, reliable and enjoyable experiences across ride-sharing, bike and scooter sharing as the future of mobility. TaaS or Mobility as a Service (MaaS) is estimated to potentially save each US family $5,600 annually on transportation cost by 2030 equivalent to a wage raise of 10%, and contribute to cleaner, safer, and more integrated communities. RethinkX Research believes that TaaS will provide 95% of the passenger miles traveled within 10 years of the widespread regulatory approval of autonomous vehicles (AVs). This assumption paints a picture of virtually little or no public mass transit expansion within the next quarter century.

In its IPO filing, Lyft claimed 46% of its riders use their cars less because of Lyft's service offerings, 35% do not own or lease a personal vehicle, and 44% of rides started or ended in low-income areas in 2018. The company claimed that an estimated 300,000 plus Lyft riders have given up their personal vehicles.

The future of mobility will make it difficult for taxis to compete, given the current trend in which ride-share companies are almost wiping them out. Then there's the added efficiency of UberX over taxis, with substantially higher capacity utilization rates in most cities studied except New York, where the utilization rates are similar.

Lyft proudly announced that its longest ride was a 639 mile (1,028.37 km) trip from Denver, CO to Sioux City, IA in 2016. I've driven three such long rides (between 100 miles [160.93 km] and 200 miles [321.87 km]) and returned home covering the same distance but without another paying passenger. The VMT cost to the driver and that to the public makes such long rides unprofitable and should be out of scope for ridesharing in the future of mobility unless costs can be balanced.

New York City transportation consultant Bruce Schaller advocates for an expansion of space-efficient and active transportation options but focuses only on one particular way for people to share rides: frequent, reliable, safe, and comfortable public transportation. Car ownership in most of America's largest cities appears to have increased from 2012, when Uber first launched its most popular ride-sharing offering UberX in cities across the US, to 2017. Ownership increasing faster than population growth reversed a trend from 2000 to 2012 when public transit ridership increased, while car ownership grew slowly. That growth has also been linked to a drop in transit ridership among some low income communities.

The United Nations projects increases in urbanization, with 68% of the world's population projected to live in cities by 2050. This represents a 55% increase from May 2018 levels, so effective and modernized mass transit systems must be central to the long-term planning for these cities of the future. Unfortunately, since 2012 when UberX launched there has been a decrease in ridership of public mass transit systems in New York City, America's largest city.

Fig. 26: Changes in total ridership by mode NYC, 2012 to 2016 (Schaller Consulting). Printed with permission

a) 2013   b) 2014

a) 2015   b) 2016

An Uber commissioned ERG study revealed that its rider's reported 1 in 10 trips connects to a bus or rail line, demonstrating that there are future opportunities for both ride- sharing and public transportation to integrate their services for a more efficient customer experience. UberPOOL accounts for 20% of Uber trips, while Lyft claims that 223 million (22.3%) of the first billion Lyft rides were shared through Lyft Line for which they deserve credit for pioneering the shared ride offering. Interestingly, 42% of UberPOOL drivers really don't like the service, compared to 15% for Lyft Line drivers (31% of Lyft Line drivers feel somewhat satisfied with the service).

Since both companies are counting on these services as the carbon-friendly traffic-decongesting future of mobility, the numbers show that Uber has room to improve with its driver partners on the value of UberPOOL. I personally hate UberPOOL because of the multiple stops and low-earnings, and I always have it turned off except when in surge zones. According to Schaller Consulting, UberX and Lyft put 2.6 new TNC vehicle miles on the road for each mile of personal autos taken off the road, for an overall 180 percent increase in driving on city streets with UberPOOL and Lyft Line shared rides making a small difference.

Lyft claims to be the "world's largest voluntary purchasers of carbon offsets" and boasts a dramatic reduction in carbon emissions since all Lyft rides are carbon neutral. The company reported a significant number of individuals who took their first ride in 2015 (an aggregate of 25.1 million rides) and whose use of the platform jumped 266% in 2018 (an aggregate of 66.9 million rides).

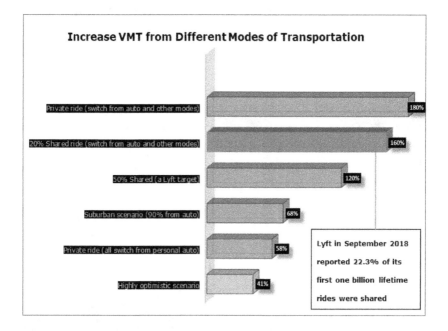

Fig. 27: Impact of TNC private ride and shared ride trips on VMT Based on Schaller Consulting data and data on Lyft's Blog.

In its best-case scenario, TNCs are likely to increase VMT by close to 50% or more. Private-ride TNC services (UberX, Lyft) put 2.8 new vehicle miles on the road for each mile of personal driving removed, for an overall 180% increase in driving on city streets.

The future of mobility must address climate change and carbon offsets are one way of addressing that issue, but the most effective method will be reducing the number of automobiles on the roads, while expanding public transport and mass transit with non-fossil dependent engines. It is worth mentioning that air transport, which is a major contributor to climate change, is also the safest means of transportation. Significant research and development must continue in that area, since it will remain an integral part of the future of mobility in a more globalized economy. There were no commercial passenger jet fatalities in 2017, making it "the safest year for aviation ever."

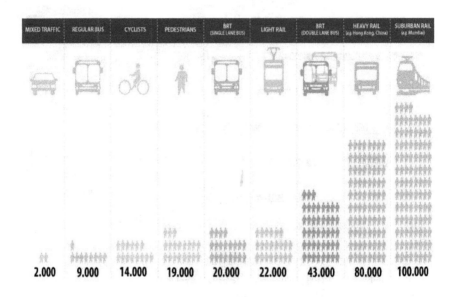

Fig. 28: Use of space and efficiency of different travel modes in cities. (Asian Development Bank, ADB, 2012).

Public and mass transit are still the most efficient means to move tens of thousands of people in large cities.

City redesigns and major road changes may well be needed necessary in any future mobility that will probably still depend heavily on cars. Such redesigns should be sensitive to how streets operate, which hours of the day are congested, which peak periods of intensity have what value, and seek a balance between needs and functions of such different time periods. Special lanes will have to be constructed for autonomous vehicles (for platooning) in the early stages, while other lanes could be expanded with accommodation for bikes, e-scooters and pedestrians. In our current route networks and systems, future autonomous taxis will face the following challenges:

1. Given bad weather, "heavy snow, rain, fog and sandstorms can obstruct the view of cameras" and lane lines maybe obscured making it difficult for these cars to auto- pilot which is why most self-driving cars are currently being tested in warm weather in Arizona and California. There are some tests being done in Pittsburg though.

2. Variations in pavement lines and presence or absence of curbs across the globe make it harder for these cars to easily navigate. Making safe left turns in the absence of a solid green arrow is as challenging to these cars as it is to human drivers.

3. Sharing space with humans on the road make for unpredictability that may result in humans assaulting these robotic cars or the cars stopping suddenly in response to human behaviors.

Electric powered trains are central to Europe's interconnectedness, with France's TGV holding a record speed of 357.2 mph (574.86 km/h) set in April 2007. Emerging Asian economies are investing heavily in these high-speed trains and China is fast connecting all its major cities, but the United States lags behind. The future of high-speed trains in the US looks bleak, even with more friendly train usage in the Northeast. California just bailed out of its high-speed train project because the cost had more than doubled due to the price of purchasing the valuable real estate between cities combined with land owners' ability to use the court system to achieve their demands. Top down and bottom up bottlenecks, including challenges to eminent domain, are cited as reasons why high speed-trains aren't likely to be part of the future of U.S., at least in the near term. I'm keeping my finger crossed that somehow the Houston to Dallas high-speed train project will defy the odds and come to fruition.

Uber Elevate is the aerial ride-sharing project that plans to scale urban air mobility (UAM) through electric vertical take-off & landing (eVTOL) aircrafts. These machines carry one pilot and four passengers, traveling at about 150 mph (241.4 km/h) for up to three hours at a cost of about $0.50 per mile traveled and landing on vertiports connecting suburbs and cities. Other companies are working on larger capacities. With electric distributed propulsion systems replacing the internal combustion engines (ICE) in helicopters, the company believes these eVTOLs will be more efficient, safer, less costly and less noisy. Early studies show that at full capacity, eVTOLs beat ground-based transport in both gasoline and electric cars, for trips of 62 miles (100 km) in the energy use, greenhouse gas (GHG) emissions, and time savings. These aircrafts may be good for the climate in the future but will come with a good deal of traffic management challenges.

Ferries and boats make up a limited means of current inland transportation mostly in cities like New York in the US, but ships, rail and freight by air still carry the bulk of goods between production, distribution and sale sites. China, through its $1 trillion Belt and Road Initiative (BRI), is building rail, roads and ports that retrace the ancient Silk Road used for trading in Asia and Europe plus a new expanded Maritime Silk Road and it is estimated to reduce the time for a shipment from China to Central Europe by more than half once completed, and at comparable or lower cost.

Cost to the community will also play a significant role in the future of mobility. Innisfil, a Canadian town with a population of about 37,000 contracted Uber-as-public-transit service for its transit needs. It spent about $150,000 ($5.62 per trip) to partially subsidize those rides while passengers paid between $3 and $5 to use the service in the pilot phase of the partnership in 2017. That spending escalated to $640,000 in 2018, and for 2019, it has allocated another $900,000. In the short-term, the 24 hour a day door-to-door service offered to any of its residents compared to using an equivalent door-to-door bus service where they will have to build an infrastructure and acquire assets like buses, saves the City some money. Via is contracted with Arlington, TX for most of that city's public transportation needs. As I pointed out in an earlier chapter, Arlington is the largest city in the United States (population 396,407) without mass transit, where each Via ride costs the rider $3 and the City and the Federal Government (federal transit administration funds) subsidize more than 50% of the total cost of the ride. Another Canadian town, Belleville, took advantage of its existing infrastructure and assets to build a hybrid on-demand AI-based technology to help restructure and run its bus system. The outcome is an increase in ridership, with each ride costing the agency a total of less than $4 compared to the more expensive Arlington and Innisfil models.

The cost to the community can also be evaluated according to who uses or needs mobility. Governing magazine analyzed Census data and found that public transportation users in U.S. cities with the 100 most public transportation commuters tend to be disproportionately poorer than those driving alone to work, and their reported median earnings was $4,314 lower. Only 45% of them had a vehicle available, and in large cities they tend to be disproportionately people of color. People served by commuter rail are wealthier than in years past while bus riders are poorer. In Dallas, almost 22% of public transportation commuters live in poverty, which is more than twice the rate for all the city's workers. What this means is that the future of mobility must ultimately include public transportation and will have to be driven in part by public policy that addresses the needs of these different communities.

Mammoth TNCs like Uber, Didi and Lyft will thrive if they continue to innovate and find new ways to become profitable while investing in the interests of all stakeholders, including their most valuable and only direct customer-facing end-user operators, their partner drivers. These companies have lured thousands of drivers onto their platforms by making their work flexible with on-demand scheduling that the driver completely controls, except when enticed by surge pricing or other promotions.

Uber understands that 16% of all U.S. workers (includes a third of workers in the retail, wholesale, and food services industries) have irregular schedules that vary based on their employers' needs. Some receive their hours one day or less in advance. This makes a predictable, flexible part-time scheduled alternative allowing them to seek additional employment and supplement their incomes at any hour of every day by signing onto and off work at their own discretion and on their own time both attractive and sustainable in any future work model.

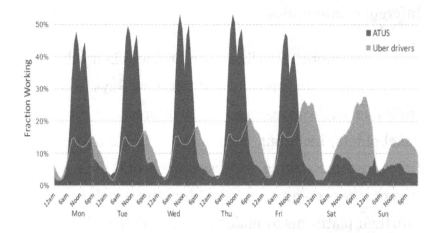

Fig. 29: How Times Uber Drivers Work Compare to Conventional Working Hours (Chen et al., 2017). Printed with permission.

American Time Use Survey (ATUS) data compared to Uber Driver data shows that many Uber drivers work conventional hours as well, but a significant number of them work non-conventional hours, especially working on weekends.

Uber acknowledges that its "business would be adversely affected if drivers were classified as employees instead of independent contractors." The Unemployment Insurance Appeal Board of New York State in July 2018 ruled that Uber drivers are employees. Other notable judicial cases in this regard include:

1. Dynamex Operations West, Inc. v. Superior Court (Filed 04/30/2018): California Supreme Court's decision establishing a new standard for determining employee or independent contractor status in the context of California wage orders.

2. Aslam, Farrar, Hoy and Mithu v. Uber BV, et al.: UK Employment Appeal Tribunal (EAT) ruled that Uber drivers are workers (rather than self- employed).

3. French Supreme Court has ruled that a driver for a third-party meal delivery service is under a "subordinate relationship" of the service, indicating an employment relationship.

4. Razak v. Uber Technologies, Inc.: US Third Circuit Court of Appeals is reviewing a summary judgment order in favor of Uber against UberBLACK Drivers in Philadelphia.

Uber's defense in the UK case as reported by Inc., exposes the operational model used by ride-share companies:

"that the driver enters into a binding agreement with a person whose identity he does not know (and will never know) and who does not know and will never know his identity, to undertake a journey to a destination not told to him until the journey begins, by a route prescribed by a stranger to the contract [Uber] from which he is not free to depart (at least not without risk), for a fee which (a) is set by the stranger, and (b) is not known by the passenger (who only is told the total to be paid), (c) is calculated by the stranger (as a percentage of the total sum) and (d) is paid to the stranger."

This is exactly how the tripartite transaction between the driver, TNC and the passenger works for Uber and Lyft drivers, but I envision a future of mobility where a ride-sharing driver is told the passenger's destination upfront, no strings attached, upon receiving a request. This would allow the driver time to make a value judgment as to whether they want to engage in that transaction as opposed to the current model where the driver is blinded to the passengers' destination (s).

Uber is already aware of this and its new Uber Pro feature takes a step to try to address it. However, like anything Uber, and in order to help commit drivers and manage its high attrition rates, the driver must attain a certain number of completed trips serviced at a certain quality level before they can unlock these benefits.

The basic level Uber Pro just offers ongoing promotions, including 1.5% cash back on gas, to all partners. The gas discount escalates to 5% at all gas stations (6.5% at Exxon/ Mobil) once the driver attains the Diamond level using a special Uber Partner Business Card from Gobank. Any charges to the card gets deducted before driver receives wages. The levels then increase to Gold, Platinum and Diamond requiring 200, 500, and 1000 completed trips in a 3-month period respectively. The Gold level driver can see the direction and estimated time of trips before accepting. The other two high- up levels also have this benefit but the Diamond level gets faster pickups at select airports and that includes the Dallas market.

In addition to accruing points to attain these top three levels, by the end of each 3-month period drivers must maintain a 4.85 star rating or above, cancel not more than 4% of requests accepted, and also maintain a 85% acceptance rate or above for incoming ride requests.

The future of mobility must treat drivers as employees, workers or quasi-employees with some essential guaranteed social benefits, rather than the current independent contractor status exploited by ride-hailing giants like Uber, Lyft and Amazon, which results in a huge burden on these individuals, their local communities and states. Such guarantees should consider standards already applied to other corporations: minimum wage, employee benefits, social security contributions, taxes, overtime, meals and rest period requirements, and penalties.

Late in 2018, New York City Taxi and Limousine Commission (TLC) mandated Uber and Lyft to pay their drivers at least $17.22/hour after expenses ($26.51/hour before expenses). Uber has announced a variable "roaming charge" fare hike based on time and distance to mitigate impending revenue losses. A congestion surcharge fee of $2.75 (calculated based on utilization rates) per passenger will be collected for the Metropolitan Transportation Authority.

Many of these transportation network companies are also in the business of developing and testing self-driving cars for a future deployment of autonomous taxis (robo-taxis) as an alternative to humans performing these tasks. The idea looked like science fiction a few years back and still scares many people today but it is viable and probably inevitable. Companies like Google's Waymo and Uber are already actively testing these cars, and other hybrid systems like Tesla's autopilot are already on the road, helping drive the car even with the driver in it. In my mind, it's just a matter of time before the public grows accustomed to this phenomenon, which is poised to become an integrated part of the human evolution. Waymo launched its Waymo One program at the end of 2018 to give customers rides in self-driving vehicles 24 hours a day in limited U.S. cities.

Goldman Sachs estimated that at the peak of autonomous car saturation, America's professional drivers could lose up to 25,000 jobs a month. There are, however, significant environmental, economic, social and safety benefits that the driverless car revolution will bring when used as taxis in the future. Autonomous Taxis are forecasted to lower greenhouse gas (GHG) emissions on a per-mile basis for driverless cars deployed as taxis, compared to conventionally driven vehicle (CDV) levels between 2014 and 2030, and projected 2030 hybrid vehicle levels.

A number of relevant technologies are in their early stages of development and most predicted benefits will be achieved at nearly full automation or SAE Levels 4 and 5. These vehicles will be accessible and convenient, customizable and will ultimately reduce cost. Uber and Lyft have perched their future profitability on automated mobility services using electric sedans. According to VTPI, total cost of ownership (TCO) is predicted to drop from $0.85 per mile in 2018 to about $0.35 per mile by 2035. That's half the $0.75 average personal TCO and operating cost for the average car in the US in 2018.

The per-mile greenhouse gas (GHG) emissions of an electric vehicle deployed as a self- driving, or autonomous taxi (AT) in 2030 would be 63-82% lower than a hybrid vehicle driven as a privately owned car that same year, and 90 percent lower than a 2014 gasoline-powered vehicle (internal combustion engine vehicle, ICEV) also driven as a privately owned car the same year (Greenblatt and Saxena, 2015). Customization or right-sizing, which means deploying the right taxi car size tailored to each trip's occupant and their specific needs, will account for almost half of the savings.

These smart cars are equipped with a range of sensors such as radar, video and laser rangefinders, a GPS unit, as well as a navigation system that processes and integrates several inputs within seconds to make a responsive decision as they drive in the community of cars, pedestrians and other road users. This computing capability, along with deep learning, machine learning and artificial intelligence, are the backbone technologies powering the driverless car revolution.

Uber's Advanced Technologies Group (ATG), in partnership with Carnegie Mellon University, developed and tested self-driving vehicles that drove one million autonomous miles in 100 days, an average of 80K miles/week. There are inherent risks in the initial phases of transitioning to driverless cars. Case in point: a fatal car accident in Tempe, AZ in March 2017 in which an Uber self-driving car with a human safety driver inside struck and killed a female pedestrian who was walking with her bicycle on the street. That is believed to be the first pedestrian death associated with self-driving technology, presenting a major setback to the belief by most researchers that self-driving cars will ultimately be safer than their human-driven counterparts.

Proponents of this argument believe that the safety of a community as a whole will eventually override any individual's zeal to claim their right to operate a car even when at risk to them or to the community. Take speeding for example, which is a leading cause of fatal accidents that ultimately cost the community through loss of life, emergency response services, hospital treatment and long-term rehabilitation care. It simply makes sense to impose and enforce speed limits in the interest of community safety or our safety as a herd (herd safety). That makes the case for a less error-prone AI-based automated driverless car network system once attainable. Such measures will inevitably be challenged unless they are made enforceable through public policy strongly supported with scientific evidence.

Autonomous cars will eventually bring down the cost of each ride significantly. Uber and Lyft will be expected to lower fares, since the cars can be on the road 24 hours a day.

This is in contrast to ride-sharing cars with drivers who currently have a maximum 12-hour drive time and a mandatory six-hour break before driving again. The predicted costs still leave significant room for humans in the future of vehicle automation as autonomous vehicles (AV) are predicted to cost less than human-driven taxis and ride- hailing services, but more than human-driven personal vehicles (HV) and public transit services according to VTPI, as shown in Fig. 30.

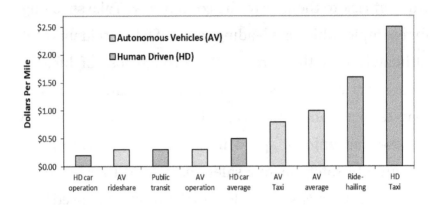

Fig. 30: Future costs of autonomous vehicles versus human-driven cars (Victoria Transport Policy Institute, VTPI). Printed with permission.

Uber's competition in autonomous technologies include Cruise Automation, Apple, Zoox, Aptiv, May Mobility, Pronto.ai, Aurora, and Nuro. As of 2017, Car2Go (owned by Daimler, the parent company of Mercedes), was "the largest car-sharing company in the world with 2.5 million registered members and a fleet of nearly 14,000 vehicles in 26 locations in North America, Europe, and Asia." DriveNow, owned by BMW, "operates over 6,000 vehicles in nine European countries, and operates as ReachNow in three U.S. cities."

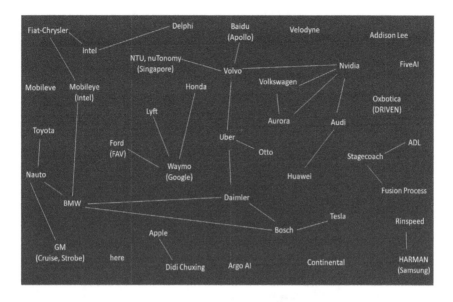

Fig. 31: Corporate partnerships between automobile industry giants and tech firms in the quest to dominate the future of driverless cars.

Trips of less than three miles (4.83 km) accounted for 46% of all U.S. vehicle trips in 2017. As an Uber driver, I generally hate non-surging short trips because the compensation is not commensurate with the time and effort input. Uber and Lyft seem to be addressing this common driver complaint by the entering the GPS-enabled dockless e-bike and e-scooter markets in major cities. These alternatives could easily become a significant consumer choice for getting from point A to point B in future mobility scenarios as I already see a trend when I drive through Downtown Dallas. Biking and walking are environmentally, the friendliest means of transportation.

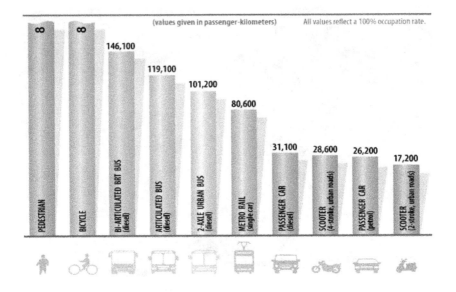

Fig. 32: Carbon dioxide (CO2) and greenhouse gas emissions from different travel modes at 100% occupancy rate. (ADB, 2012)

Walking and bicycling put negligible CO2 into the atmosphere.

Future competition to established giants like Uber and Lyft will ultimately benefit local communities and certain niches/specific markets by addressing and offering solutions to weaknesses in the practices and policies of those giants. They won't, or shouldn't repeat mistakes like not treating their drivers as employees, as well as safety and reliability issues.

Take Alto for example, a Dallas startup that classifies its drivers as employees with benefits. Alto is also a TaaS ride-sharing company with a monthly subscription fee that gives its riders the in-app opportunity to set what kind of in-car experience they will like on options like having no conversation with the driver and the type of music mix, thus giving the rider that ability to customize their ride. When self-driving cars eventually dominate the personal mobility space, a niche will remain for people who don't feel comfortable in a driverless car or may simply want a human driver for conversational purposes. Uber reported in 2018 that 14% of its trips in the U.S. allowed riders to visit destinations they could not access without Uber, meaning that in the future of mobility, a market will remain for ride-sharing where public transit falls short.

Current statistics still favor human drivers in real life over the utopian system of exclusively driverless cars circulating with less chance of error or accident. Some estimates put human safety performance at 10,000 better than the current self-driving car which fails or disengages roughly every 10,000 miles (16,093.44 km). The consequence of this could be a fatality, as discussed earlier, while humans collectively drive about 100 million miles (160.93 million kilometers) before causing a fatality and 10 million miles (16.93 million kilometers) before an injury-causing accident.

Applying Moore's Law such that these cars double their performance every 16 months or so, it will still be the 2030s before safe circulation and societal comfort are established. However, with Waymo One now an operating self-driving taxi service in select cities, there is the possibility of a dramatic improvement in the technology that just might bring driverless cars to pick you up when you call for a ride in the next few years.

In 2017, there were 10,874 U.S. fatalities in motor vehicle traffic crashes involving drivers with blood alcohol concentrations (BACs) of.08 g/dL or higher, representing 29% of all traffic fatalities for the year. The 21 to 24 year-old age group had the highest percentage (27%). Lyft makes the argument that the number of teenagers getting their driver licenses by age 18 is trending downward; consequently, alongside savings on parking, insurance and car payments, there remain growth opportunities for increasing ride-sharing usage.

NHTSA estimates the economic cost of all alcohol-impaired accidents in the U.S. in 2010 was $44 billion. The DFW Metroplex led Texas in 2017 with the most DUI (alcohol) involved crashes. Dallas ranked third in that category, but second in total crashes and injuries statewide with 50,627. The most statewide DUIs occurred between 9 PM and 3 AM. Twenty-one-year-olds had the highest rate of fatalities and young people aged 21 to 27 caused almost 35% of all fatalities among drivers aged 16 to 44.

Many of these young Millennials tend to party on weekend nights in the Dallas bar districts where I usually seek customers. The majority of them use ride-sharing to get back home after a night of excessive drinking. Dallas was once ranked as the city with the most drunk driving deaths nationwide, with 10.23 deaths per 100,000 residents per year.

Uber and Lyft tout studies showing a drop in alcohol-related fatalities from motor vehicle crashes when ride sharing is available in certain markets, but they criticize limited studies that indicate an increase in overall crashes after ride sharing enters the market. These companies have incident and crash reports they can and should make available to researchers to help the public better understand the trends.

Uber's Law Enforcement web portal "enables law enforcement to access trip data and other information that may be critical for solving criminal cases quickly and securely." Safety must also be built in and to that end, Uber just incorporated in-app safety menu options in Ride Check and Safety Toolkit for drivers and riders to use in ride verification, reporting safety issues or contacting law enforcement.

The future of mobility must include partnerships between the private and public sectors for effective, efficient and low-cost movement of people, goods and services. Uber Movement helps urban planners, local leaders, and civic communities make informed decisions about their cities. Airports are being forced to make accommodations for ride- sharing drivers and both Uber and Lyft are allocating special pickup areas in major events arena and stadium. The future of mobility will rely on well-designed cities with mass transit around such venues. In a partnership with Masabi, Uber is testing its app for public-transit ticketing and other integrations to facilitate public transportation. Future mobility will benefit from the expertise of such technologies.

As our future cities continue to grow denser, the future of mobility will require a comprehensive and systematic approach to harness and effectively and efficiently utilize the different means of transportation I've described in this book. I will not be surprised if at some point in the future, humans simply transform themselves as necessary and use whatever form of transportation they choose to get from Point A to Point B, as commonly depicted in superhero movies. AI tracks and modulates our behavioral patterns to help organize and facilitate our life activities, including mobility. Maybe CRISPR or some future technology will actually modify our inherent (genetic) abilities so humans can simply tap into that capability and transform or transport themselves as they wish.

Fig. 33: Self-transforming Transportation Modes

ACKNOWLEDGMENTS

This book is the product of being challenged by artificial intelligence, AI. It is thanks to Uber's control and manipulation of its partner drivers that this research work came to fruition. It is also thanks to Uber's pursuit of an IPO which forced the company to dump many of the information covered in this book. Though much of the research had been done before both Uber and Lyft filed their IPO prospectus, the work in this book is validated by that which both companies have made public.

A lot of the book's design was gradually developed over two years since I started driving for Uber. Personal accounts and receipts were carefully mapped and documented. However, without Uber's S-1 filing with the Securities and Exchange Commission, some of the stories would have had second hand references. Uber's public confirmation of most of the stories strengthens the case made in the book.

The brain behind publishing this separate "geek and analyst" book is its visionary editor, Mrs. Betsy Gilbert who had the foresight to break up my original manuscript into three to not overwhelm ride-share consumers who simply want the juicy stories from my experiences. Several phone calls and drafts between us led to this final product which we hope the target audience appreciates.

I must also acknowledge the several original authors who granted me permission to reproduce or use their work within short notice. Based only on the limited knowledge that I was "writing a book on ride-sharing," these benevolent authors generously allowed me to use their work and for that I am grateful. I am especially grateful to Bruce Schaller of Schaller Consulting. There was no effort made to get Uber involved with the book. Instead, all research was done independent of Uber and Lyft's knowledge to uphold the integrity of the book and its work.

NOTES

1."16 Billion Ride-Hailing Trips Completed Globally in 2017 - 24 BillionTrips Expected in 2018." ABI Research: for Visionaries, www.abiresearch.com/press/16-billion-ride-hailing-trips-completed-globally-2017-24-billion-tripsexpected-2018/.

2."2017 Safest Year for Air Travel as Fatalities Fall." BBC News, BBC, 2Jan. 2018, www.bbc.com/news/business-42538053.

3."2018 Uber and Lyft Driver Survey Results – The Rideshare Guy." TheRideshare Guy Blog and Podcast, 14 Mar. 2019, therideshareguy.com/2018-uber-and-lyft-driver-survey-results-the-rideshare-guy/.

4."A Computer Called Watson." IBM100 - A Computer Called Watson, www.ibm.com/ibm/history/ibm100/us/en/icons/watson/.

5."A Timeline of Uber's Rough Year." Fox Business, Fox Business, 21June 2017, www.foxbusiness.com/features/atimeline-of-ubers-rough-year.

6."Autonomous Taxis Would Deliver Significant Environmental andEconomic Benefits." ScienceDaily, ScienceDaily, 6 July 2015, www.sciencedaily.com/releases/2015/07/150706114135.htm.

7."Average Annual Miles per Driver by Age Group." U.S. Department ofTransportation/Federal Highway Administration, www.fhwa.dot.gov/ohim/onh00/bar8.htm.

8."Electric Aircraft Will Help Save The World." CleanTechnica, 6 May2019, cleantechnica.com/2019/05/06/electricaircraft-will-help-save-the-world/.

9."Evolution's Next Step: A.I." (2018, March 27). Think, KERA.Retrieved February 23, 2019 from http://think.kera.org/2018/03/27/evolutions-next-step-a-i/

10."Executive Summary." U.S. Department of Transportation/FederalHighway Administration, www.fhwa.dot.gov/policy/2010cpr/execsum.cfm.

11."Facts Statistics: Auto Insurance." III, www.iii.org/fact-statistic/facts-statistics-auto-insurance.

12."Generations X,Y, Z and the Others." WJSchroer,socialmarketing.org/archives/generations-xy-z-and-the-others/.

13."Highway Functional Classification Concepts, Criteria and Procedures."U.S. Department of Transportation/Federal Highway Administration, www.fhwa.dot.gov/planning/processes/statewide/related/highway_functional_classifications/section00.cfm.

14."How Belleville, Ont., Is Using Technology to Tackle Transit Troubles |CBC News." CBCnews, CBC/Radio Canada, 4 Oct. 2018, www.cbc.ca/news/thenational/how-belleville-ont-is-using-technology-to-tackle-transit-troubles-1.4849946.

15."In-Depth Guide to the Lyft IPO - Transportation Disruptor or MoneyPit?" Grizzle, 6 May 2019, grizzle.com/lyftipotransportation-disruptor-money-pit/.

16. "Integrating Economics with Psychology." The Committee for the Prizein Economic Sciences in Memory of Alfred Nobel. The Royal Swedish Academy of Sciences. October 9, 2017

17. "Introducing Uber Pro." Uber. https://www.uber.com/us/en/drive/uber-pro/

18. "IRS Issues Standard Mileage Rates for 2019." Internal RevenueService, www.irs.gov/newsroom/irs-issues-standardmileage-rates-for-2019.

19. "Les Dames Européennes a La Promenade Du Soir En Hamac AuxEnvirons De Ouidah (Bas-Dahomey)." NYPL Digital Collections, digitalcollections.nypl.org/items/510d47df-9d59-a3d9-e040-e00a18064a99.

20. "Lyft Revenue and Usage Statistics (2019)." Business of Apps, 29 Apr.2019, www.businessofapps.com/data/lyftstatistics/.

21. "Re-Designing Public Transit to Meet Today's Needs." Pantonium,pantonium.com/re-designing-public-transit-to-meet-todays-needs/.

22. "Reported List Of Incidents Involving Uber And Lyft." AtchisonTransport Services, 26 June 2018, www.atchisontransport.com/blog/reported-list-of-incidents-involving-uber-and-lyft/.

23. "Safari Live - Day 226." (2018, September 16). National Geographic.Retrieved January 20, 2019 from https://www.youtube.com/watch?v=uKJeFaUMgJQ

24. "Taxi Insurance 101." Taxi Insurance HQ,www.taxiinsurancehq.com/taxi-insurance-cost/.

25. "Technological Intuition." Think, KERA. (2015, September 23).Retrieved February 23, 2019 from think.kera.org/2015/09/23/technological-intuition/.

26. "TGV, Maglev, Bullet - Our Top Five High-Speed Trains! - CBBCNewsround." BBC News, BBC, www.bbc.co.uk/newsround/21229721.

27. "The 15 Most Dangerous Jobs In America." Business Insider, 11 Mar.2010, www.businessinsider.com/the-15-mostdangerous-jobs-in-america-2010-3.

28. "The Online Platform Economy in 2018 | JPMorgan Chase Institute."JPMorgan Chase & Co., www.jpmorganchase.com/corporate/institute/report-ope-2018.htm.

29. "This Dallas Startup Just Hauled in $14.5 Million to Disrupt Uber,Lyft." Dallas News, 22 Jan. 2019. www.dallasnews.com/business/entrepre-neurs/2019/01/22/dallas-startup-just-hauled- 145-million-disrupt-uber-lyft

30. "Traffic Volume Trends". US Dept. of Transportation. Federal HighwayAdministration. December 2018. https://www.fhwa.dot.gov/policyinformation/travel_monitoring/18dectvt/18dectvt.pdf

31. "Uber Agrees to Pay $20 Million to Settle FTC Charges That ItRecruited Prospective Drivers with Exaggerated Earnings Claims." Federal Trade Commission, 23 Jan. 2017, www.ftc.gov/news-events/press-releases/2017/01/uberagrees-pay-20-million-settle-ftc-charges-it-recruited.

32. "Uber Elevate Wrangles Electric Aircraft Leaders To Shake OffNegative Public Image." CleanTechnica, 13 May 2018,

cleantechnica.com/2018/05/13/uber-elevate-wrangles-electric-aircraft-leaders-to-shake-off-negative-public-image/.

33."Uber IPO 2019: After Lyft IPO, Uber IPO Released And BecomePublicly Traded Company -Thu May 16." Oofy, 16 May 2019, theoofy.com/42941/uber-ipo-date-after-lyft-ipo-time-has-come-for-uber-to-become-a-publicly-tradedcompany-fri-apr-26/.

34."Uber Organizational Structure - Research-Methodology." Research, 6Mar. 2018, research-methodology.net/uberorganizational-structure-3/.

35."Uber Report: Eric Holder's Recommendations for Change." The NewYork Times, The New York Times, 13 June 2017, www.nytimes.com/2017/06/13/technology/uber-report-eric-holders-recommendations-for-change.html.

36."Uber Revenue and Usage Statistics (2019)." Business of Apps, 10 May2019, www.businessofapps.com/data/uberstatistics/.

37."Uber Services Suspended in Barcelona." BBC News, BBC, 31 Jan.2019, www.bbc.com/news/business-47071710.

38."United States Labor Force Statistics - Seasonally Adjusted." DLT,www.dlt.ri.gov/lmi/laus/us/usadj.htm.

39."What Are Genome Editing and CRISPR-Cas9? - Genetics HomeReference - NIH." U.S. National Library of Medicine, National Institutes of Health, ghr.nlm.nih.gov/primer/genomicresearch/genomeediting.

40."What Lyft's New $600 Million Investment Means For the Ride-Hailing Wars." Fortune, fortune.com/2018/06/28/lyftfunding-fidelity/.

41."Who Uses Public Transportation in Your City?" Governing,www.governing.com/gov-data/transportationinfrastructure/public-transportation-demographics-ridership-data-for-cities.html.

42."Will EVTOL Aircraft Pollute More Or Less Than Road Cars In TheComing Urban Mobility Future?" CleanTechnica, 13 Apr. 2019, cleantechnica.com/2019/04/13/will-evtol-aircraft-pollute-more-or-less-than-road-cars-in-the-comingurban-mobility-future/.

43."Your Driving Costs." AAA NewsRoom,newsroom.aaa.com/auto/your-driving-costs/.

44.180 Days of Change. Uber. Retrieved January 17, 2019 fromhttps://www.uber.com/c/180-days/summary/

45.2017 safest year for air travel as fatalities fall. BBC News, BBC, 2018,January 2. Retrieved April 21, 2019 from https://www.bbc.com/news/business-42538053

46.Adams, T. (2017, June 4). Surge pricing comes to the supermarket. TheGuardian. Retrieved January 20, 2019 from https://www.theguardian.com/technology/2017/jun/04/surge-pricing-comes-to-the-supermarket-dynamic-personal-data

47.Alderman, L. (2017, December 20). Uber Dealt Setback After EuropeanCourt Rules It Is a Taxi Service. New York Times. Retrieved January 20, 2019 from https://www.nytimes.com/2017/12/20/business/uber-europe-ecj.html

48.Ananthaswamy, A. (2012, August 6). Brain might not stand in the way of free will. Newscientist. Retrieved January 24, 2019 from https://www.newscientist.com/article/dn22144-brain-might-not-stand-in-the-way-of-free-will/

49.Asian Development Bank. "Solutions for Urban Transport." AsianDevelopment Bank, Asian Development Bank, 18 Dec. 2017, www.adb.org/news/infographics/solutions-urban-transport.

50.Asociación Profesional Elite Taxiv Uber Systems Spain, SL. Case C-434/15 (2017, May 11). https://curia.europa.eu/jcms/upload/docs/application/pdf/2017-05/cp170050en.pdf

51.Auchard, Eric. "Uber Re-Enters Barcelona with Professional DriverService." Reuters, Thomson Reuters, 13 Mar. 2018, www.reuters.com/article/us-uber-europe-barcelona/uber-re-enters-barcelona-with-professional-driver-serviceidUSKCN1GO2V7.

52.Baker, David R. "Partner up! Self-Driving Car Firms Form TangledWeb of Alliances." SFChronicle.com, San Francisco Chronicle, 20 May 2017, www.sfchronicle.com/business/article/Partner-up-Self-driving-car-firms-formtangled-11160522.php.

53.Balakrishnan, Anita. "Self-Driving Cars Could Cost America'sProfessional Drivers up to 25,000 Jobs a Month, Goldman Sachs Says." CNBC, 22 May 2017, www.cnbc.com/2017/05/22/goldman-sachs-analysis-of-autonomousvehicle-job-loss.html.

54.Banerjee, A. V. (1992). A Simple Model of Herd Behavior. TheQuarterly Journal of Economics, Vol. CVII August 1992, Issue 3. Retrieved January 18, 2019 from https://economics.mit.edu/files/8869

55.Banerjee, Siddhartha and Riquelme, Carlos and Johari, Ramesh, Pricingin Ride-Share Platforms: A Queueing-Theoretic Approach (February 10, 2015). Available at SSRN: https://ssrn.com/abstract=2568258 or http://dx.doi.org/10.2139/ssrn.2568258

56.Barreiro, S. Are Uber Drivers Employees or Independent Contractors inCalifornia? Retrieved January 20, 2019 from https://www.nolo.com/legal-encyclopedia/california-labor-commissioner-rules-uber-driver-employee-not-independentcontractor.html

57.Bash, H. (2017, March 11). Thousands Attend St. Patrick's Parade inDallas. Retrieved March 1, 2019 from https://www.nbcdfw.com/news/local/Thousands-Attend-St-Patricks-Parade-in-Dallas-415947483.html

58.Berboucha, M. (2018, May 28). Uber Self-Driving Car Crash: WhatReally Happened. Retrieved January 18, 2019 from https://www.forbes.com/sites/meriameberboucha/2018/05/28/uber-self-driving-car-crash-what-reallyhappened/#7b1640904dc4

59.Bershidsky, L. (2018, July 31). Don't blame Uber for your city'scongestion. Bloomberg. Retrieved January 17, 2019 from https://www.chicagotribune.com/news/opinion/commentary/ct-perspec-uber-blame-trac-congestion-0801-story.html

60.Bhuiyan, J. (August 20, 2017). Everything you need to know aboutUber's turbulent 2017. Retrieved January 17, 2019 from https://www.recode.net/2017/8/20/16164176/uber-2017-timeline-scandal

61.Bliss, Laura, and Laura Bliss. "'Uber Was Supposed To Be Our PublicTransit'." CityLab, 1 May 2019, www.citylab.com/transportation/2019/04/innisfil-transit-ride-hailing-bus-public-transportation-uber/588154/.

62.Bowcott, Owen. "Uber to Face Stricter EU Regulation after ECJ RulesIt Is Transport Firm." The Guardian, Guardian News and Media, 20 Dec. 2017, www.theguardian.com/technology/2017/dec/20/uber-european-court-of-justice-rulingbarcelona-taxi-drivers-ecj-eu.

63.Brewster, T. (2017, August 15). FTC: Uber Failed To Protect 100,000Drivers In 2014 Hack. Retrieved April 21, 2019 from https://www.forbes.com/sites/thomasbrewster/2017/08/15/uber-settles-ftc-complaint-over-secuirty-andprivacy/#2778bf5f88da

64.Brinklow, A. (2018, July 27). Lyft, Uber increase traffic 180 percent inmajor cities, says report: Riders are giving up public transit—not their cars—in favor of ride-hailing trips. Retrieved January 17, 2019 from https://sf.curbed.com/2018/7/27/17622178/uber-lyft-cause-traffic-streets-congestion-bruce-schaller-tnc-report

65.Brown, E. (2019, May 12). Uber and Lyft Face Hurdle of Finding andKeeping Drivers. The Wall Street Journal. Retrieved May 15, 2019 from https://www.wsj.com/articles/uber-and-lyft-face-tough-test-of-finding-and-keepingdrivers-11557673863

66.Bureau of Labor Statistics, U.S. Department of Labor, OccupationalOutlook Handbook, Taxi Drivers, Ride-Hailing Drivers, and Chauffeurs, on the Internet at https://www.bls.gov/ooh/transportation-and-material-moving/taxi-driversand-chauffeurs.htm (visited 2019, January 16).

67.Burke, M. (2019, February 5). Michigan Uber driver who murdered 6people in shooting rampage sentenced to life in prison. Retrieved February 12, 2019 from https://www.nbcnews.com/news/us-news/michigan-uber-driver-whomurdered-6-people-shooting-rampage-sentenced-n967231

68.Carson, Biz. "It's Official: Dara Khosrowshahi Is Uber's New CEO."Forbes, Forbes Magazine, 30 Aug. 2017, www.forbes.com/sites/bizcarson/2017/08/29/its-ocial-dara-khosrowshahi-is-ubers-new-ceo/#607d570c2e2f.

69.Chan, Julia. Top Ridesharing Apps Worldwide for 2018: Uber Led thePack, sensortower.com/blog/top-ridesharingapps-worldwide-2018.

70.Chappell, Bill. "Uber Pays $148 Million Over Yearlong Cover-Up OfData Breach." NPR, NPR, 27 Sept. 2018, www.npr.org/2018/09/27/652119109/uber-pays-148-million-over-year-long-cover-up-of-data-breach.

71.Cho, Y. (2018, December 8). Lyft driver arrested, accused of sexuallyassaulting a passenger. Retrieved February 12, 2019 from https://www.kxan.com/news/local/austin/lyft-driver-arrested-accused-of-sexually-assaulting-a- passenger/1646847750

72.Chowdhry, A. (2016, May 25). Uber: Users Are More Likely To PaySurge Pricing If Their Phone Battery Is Low. Retrieved January 20, 2019 from https://www.forbes.com/sites/amitchowdhry/2016/05/25/uber-lowbattery/#321ccd5574b3

73.Citation Machine. http://www.citationmachine.net/

74.Clark, K. Will Uber gobble up Lime or Fly off with Bird? Consolidationis afoot in the electric scooter market.
Retrieved January 27, 2019 from https://techcrunch.com/2018/12/03/will-uber-gobble-up-lime-or-y-o-with-bird/

75.CNN. (2018, December 17). World's most popular attractions,according to Uber. Retrieved January 24, 2019 from
https://www.cnn.com/travel/article/uber-most-popular-attractions-2018/index.html

76.Cody J Cook and Rebecca E Diamond and Jonathan Hall and John A.List and Paul E. Oyer. The Gender Earnings Gap in the Gig Economy : Evidence from over a Million Rideshare Drivers, 2018.
https://web.stanford.edu/~diamondr/UberPayGap.pdf

77.Conger, K. (2018, November 14). Uber's Losses Continue Ahead ofInitial Public Offering. Retrieved January 27, 2019 from
https://www.nytimes.com/2018/11/14/technology/uber-losses-initial-public-offering.html?module=inline

78.Constine, J. How Uber will become an ad company, starting with EatsPool. Retrieved January 18, 2019 from
https://techcrunch.com/2018/12/10/uber-ads/

79.Contract Law: What is the Dierence Between a "term" and a"condition". Retrieved January 26, 2019 from
https://boards.straightdope.com/sdmb/showthread.php?t=631522

80.Copeland, Laura, and Laura Copeland. "What You Can Make Drivingwith Lyft." Medium, Sharing the Ride with Lyft, 12 Apr. 2018,
medium.com/@lauracope/what-you-can-make-driving-with-lyft-f9a840cc20d9.

81.Cramer, Judd, and Alan B. Krueger. 2016. "Disruptive Change in theTaxi Business: The Case of Uber." American Economic Review, 106 (5): 177-82. DOI: 10.1257/aer.p20161002.

82.Crook, J. Uber applies for patent that would detect drunk passengers.Retrieved January 18, 2019 from
https://techcrunch.com/2018/06/11/uber-applies-for-patent-that-would-detect-drunk-passengers/

83.Cruz, Mayra. "Houston-Dallas High-Speed Rail Construction MayBegin in Late 2019." Houston Chronicle, 15 Feb. 2019,
www.chron.com/neighborhood/spring/news/article/Houston-Dallas-high-speed-rail-construction-may-13620560.php.

84.Culturemap. Cities. Dallas.
2018.http://dallas.culturemap.com/events/?day=17&month=3&year=2018

85.Day, M. Ending the Amazon Hunger Games. Retrieved January 18,2019 from https://jacobinmag.com/2018/02/amazon-corporate-headquarters-tax-breaks

86.DeCambre, Mark. "Uber's IPO Was the 5th Worst over the PastQuarter-Century, by This Measure." MarketWatch, 13 May 2019,
www.marketwatch.com/story/ubers-ipo-was-the-5th-worst-over-the-past-quarter-century-by-thismeasure-2019-05-10.

87.DFW International Airport Finance Department. (2018). FY 2018Schedule of Charges. Retrieved January 17, 2019 from https://www.dfwairport.com/cs/groups/webcontent/documents/webasset/p2_90 2698.pdf

88.Dillet, R. (2019, February 16). Uber sues NYC to contest cap ondrivers. Retrieved February 16, 2019 from https://techcrunch.com/2019/02/16/uber-sues-nyc-to-contest-cap-on-drivers/

89.Divine, J. (2019, January 8). 9 Major Upcoming IPOs to Watch in 2019.Retrieved March 21, 2019 from https://money. usnews.com/investing/stock-market-news/slideshows/best-stocks-ipo-this-year

90.Dowling, Savannah. "Inside The Uber S-1: Revenue, Growth, AndLosses." Crunchbase News, Crunchbase News, 11 Apr. 2019, news.crunchbase.com/news/inside-the-uber-s-1-revenue-growth-and-losses/.

91.Dudovskiy, J. (2018, March 7). Uber Organizational Structure.Retrieved February 12, 2019 from https://researchmethodology.net/uber-organizational-structure-3/

92.Economic Development Research Group (EDR Group). (2018). Uber'sEconomic Impacts in the United States. https://drive.google.com/le/d/1P6HMbPc8T91Y8NlYyFGv8NQS9g4ckAq9/view

93.Ehrenkranz, M. (2018, June 6). Uber Will Drop Up to $500 Million onAds Letting You Know How Truly Sorry It Is. Retrieved January 23, 2019 from https://gizmodo.com/uber-will-drop-up-to-500-million-on-ads-letting-you-kn-1826600829

94.Erb, K. P. (2018, December 14). IRS Announces 2019 Mileage Rates.Retrieved February 11, 2019 from https://www.forbes.com/sites/kellyphillipserb/2018/12/14/irs-announces-2019-mileage-rates/#6bdb67745e51

95.Farivar, Cyrus, and Ars Technica. "2017 4 21 Letter to Portland."DocumentCloud, www.documentcloud.org/documents/3700653-2017-4-21-Letter-to-Portland.html.

96.Farrell, D., Greig, F., & Hamoudi, A. (September 2018).The OnlinePlatform Economy in 2018. Drivers, Workers, Sellers, and Lessors. JPMorgan Chase & Co. Institute. Retrieved February 24, 2019 from https://www.jpmorganchase.com/corporate/institute/document/institute-ope-2018.pdf

97.Federal Highway Administration, U.S. Department of Transportation,Office of Highway Policy Information, Average Annual Miles per Driver by Age Group. Retrieved January 17, 2019 from

98.Federal Trade Commission, Plaintiff, v. Uber Technologies, Inc., aDelaware corporation, Defendant. Case 3:17-cv-00261. (2017). Retrieved May 15, 2019 from https://www.ftc.gov/system/files/documents/cases/1523082ubercmplt.pdf

99.Fedschun, T. Las Vegas Uber driver pummeled by passengers in attackcaught on video. Retrieved February 12, 2019 from https://www.foxnews.com/us/uber-driver-in-las-vegas-attacked-by-passengers-after-refusing-to-give-ride

100. Fitzsimmons, E. G. (2018, December 2). Why Are Taxi Drivers in New York Killing Themselves? The New York Times. Retrieved January 23, 2019 from https://www.nytimes.com/2018/12/02/nyregion/taxi-drivers-suicide-nyc.html

101. Fox-Brewster, Thomas. "FTC: Uber Failed To Protect 100,000 Drivers In 2014 Hack." Forbes, Forbes Magazine, 15 Aug. 2017, www.forbes.com/sites/thomasbrewster/2017/08/15/uber-settles-ftc-complaint-over-secuirty-andprivacy/#2778bf5f88da.

102. Gao, P., Hensley R., & Zielke A. (2014, October). A road map to the future for the auto industry. Mckinsey. Retrieved January 16, 2019, from https://www.mckinsey.com/industries/automotive-and-assembly/our-insights/a-road-map-tothe-future-for-the-auto-industry

103. Generations X,Y, Z and the Others. Retrieved January 17, 2019 from http://socialmarketing.org/archives/generationsxy-z-and-the-others/

104. Gessner, K. (2018 December 17). Rideshare: With IPOs looming, Uber leads market share, but Lyft has gained ground. Retrieved January 16, 2019, from https://blog.secondmeasure.com/2018/10/17/rideshare-industry-overview/

105. Gessner, Kathryn. "Rideshare: Uber Announces IPO, Leads Rideshare Sales over Lyft." Second Measure, 22 Apr. 2019, blog.secondmeasure.com/datapoints/rideshare-industry-overview/.

106. Goldstein, M. (2018, February 22). Uber And Lyft Pound Taxis, Rental Cars In Business Travel Market. Retrieved January 27, 2019 from https://www.forbes.com/sites/michaelgoldstein/2018/02/22/uber-and-lyft-pound-taxis-rentalcars-in-business-travel-market/#2cd6b264b5e7

107. Goodman, J. David. "Amazon Pulls Out of Planned New York City Headquarters." The New York Times, 14 Feb. 2019, www.nytimes.com/2019/02/14/nyregion/amazon-hq2-queens.html.

108. Greenblatt, Jeffery B., and Samveg Saxena. "Autonomous Taxis Could Greatly Reduce Greenhouse-Gas Emissions of US Light-Duty Vehicles." Nature News, Nature Publishing Group, 6 July 2015, www.nature.com/articles/nclimate2685.

109. Griswold, Alison, and Alison Griswold. "Uber Drivers in New York Could Earn More with This Simple Formula." Quartz, Quartz, 5 July 2018, qz.com/1320449/this-simple-formula-could-increase-pay-for-uber-drivers-in-new-york/.

110. Hall, .J. (2018, March 2). An analysis of CEEPR's Paper on "The Economics of Ride-Hailing". Uber. Retrieved January 20, 2019 from https://medium.com/uber-under-the-hood/an-analysis-of-ceeprs-paper-on-the-economics-of- ridehailing-1c8bfbf1081d

111. Hall, J., Kendrick, Cory, Nosko, C. (2015). The Effects of Uber's Surge Pricing: A Case Study. Retrieved January 20, 2019 from http://economicsforlife.ca/wp-content/uploads/2015/10/effects_of_ubers_surge_pricing.pdf

112. Hanna, Bill, and Gordon Dickson. "This Is the Largest City in U.S. without Mass Transit. Is It a Transportation Innovator?" Star, Fort Worth Star-Telegram, 4 Feb. 2019, www.star-telegram.com/news/local/community/arlington/article225196630.html.

113. Hanna, Bill. "Move People around a City without Mass Transit? This City Says They're Doing It." Star, Fort Worth Star-Telegram, 10 Dec. 2018, www.star-telegram.com/news/local/community/arlington/article222789835.html.

114. Hartmans, Avery. "Uber Says It Has over 80% of the Ride-Hailing Market in the U.S." Business Insider, 25 Aug. 2016, www.businessinsider.com/uber-majority-ride-hailing-market-share-lyft-us-2016-8?utm_source=feedly&utm_medium=webfeeds.

115. Hawkins, A. J. (2017, December 5). You can now reserve a luxury Mercedes-Benz sedan with Car2Go in NYC. The Verge. Retrieved April 21, 2019 from https://www.theverge.com/2017/12/5/16737886/car2go-daimler-mercedesbenz-nyc-car-share

116. Hawkins, A. J. (2018, April 2). BMW and Daimler are putting their differences aside to beat Uber. The Verge. Retrieved April 21, 2019 from https://www.theverge.com/2018/4/2/17188374/bmw-daimler-merger-car2go-reachnow-mobility

117. Hayes, D. R., Snow, C., & Altuwayjiri, S. (2018, March). A Dynamic and Static Analysis of the Uber Mobile Application from a Privacy Perspective. Journal of Information Systems Applied Research (JISAR) 11(1) ISSN: 1946- 1836

118. Hensley, R, Padhi, A, and Salazar, J. (2017). Cracks in the ridesharing market—and how to fill them. Retrieved February 21, 2019 from https://www.mckinsey.com/industries/automotive-and-assembly/our-insights/cracks-in-theridesharing-market-and-how-to-fill-them

119. Holder, Sarah, et al. "Why Is Lyft Fighting New York City Over Driver Pay?" CityLab, 1 Feb. 2019, www.citylab.com/transportation/2019/02/uber-lyft-taxi-minimum-wage-ride-hailing-drivers-new-york/581707/.

120. Hondorp, Kae. "1 Billion Rides. 1 Billion Connections." Lyft Blog, Lyft Blog, 18 Sept. 2018, blog.lyft.com/posts/one-billion-rides.

121. Hondorp, Kae. "Lyft Community Surpasses $10 Million in Donations." Lyft Blog, Lyft Blog, 19 Nov. 2018, blog.lyft.com/posts/lyft-community-surpasses-10-million-in-donations.

122. How Becoming Employees Could Change Things for Uber Drivers. Retrieved January 20, 2019 from https://www.ridester.com/uber-drivers-become-employees/

123. How much does it cost to build an app like Uber for iOS or Android? Quora. Retrieved January 18, 2019 from https://www.quora.com/How-much-does-it-cost-to-build-an-app-like-Uber-for-iOS-or-Android

124. Huston, C. (2017, May 27). Ride-hailing industry expected to grow eightfold to $285 billion by 2030. Retrieved March 21, 2019 from https://www.marketwatch.com/story/ride-hailing-industry-expected-to-grow-eightfold-to-285-billion-by-2030-2017-05-24

125. IBM 100. A Computer Called Watson. IBM. Retrieved March 1, 2019 from https://www.ibm.com/ibm/history/ibm100/us/en/icons/watson/

126. Ink, Social. "Design Hour." National Association of City Transportation Officials, nacto.org/publication/urban-streetdesign-guide/design-controls/design-hour/.

127. Inrix. "Congestion Costs Each American 97 Hours, $1,348 A Year." INRIX, inrix.com/press-releases/scorecard-2018-us/.

128. Introducing Uber Rewards. Uber. Retrieved January 17, 2019 from https://www.uber.com/us/en/u/rewards/

129. Irving Firemen's Relief & Retirement Fund, Individually and on Behalf of All Others Similarly Situated, Plaintiff, vs. Uber Technologies Inc. And Travis Kalanick, Defendants. Case 3:17-cv-05558. (2017). Retrieved May 15, 2019 from https://regmedia.co.uk/2017/09/26/uber-irving-lawsuit.pdf

130. Isaac Mike. "How Uber Deceives the Authorities Worldwide." The New York Times, The New York Times, 3 March 2017, https://olis.leg.state.or.us/liz/2017R1/Downloads/CommitteeMeetingDocument/114647

131. Isaac, M. (2017, April 23). Uber's C.E.O. Plays With Fire. Retrieved January 26, 2019 from https://www.nytimes.com/2017/04/23/technology/travis-kalanick-pushes-uber-and-himself-to-the-precipice.html

132. Isaac, M., Conger, K., & Griffith E. (2018, December 7). Uber Is Said to File for an I.P.O. as It Races Lyft to a Public Debut. New York Times. Retrieved January 20, 2019 from https://www.nytimes.com/2018/12/07/technology/uberipo.html

133. Isaac, Mike. "Uber Is Sued by Woman Who Was Raped by One of Its Drivers in India." The New York Times, The New York Times, 15 June 2017, www.nytimes.com/2017/06/15/technology/uber-india-rape-lawsuit.html.

134. Jabr, F. (2011, December 8). Cache Cab: Taxi Drivers' Brains Grow to Navigate London's Streets. Memorizing 25,000 city streets balloons the hippocampus, but cabbies may pay a hidden fare in cognitive skills. Scientific American. Retrieved January 18, 2019 from https://www.scientificamerican.com/article/london-taxi-memory/

135. James Arbib & Tony Seba. Rethinking Transportation 2020-2030. RethinkX Research. May 2017. https://static1.squarespace.com/static/585c3439be65942f022bbf9b/t/591a2e4be6f2e1c13df930c5/1494888038959/RethinkX+Report_051517.pdf

136. Jannarone, J. (2019, March 26). Swelling Insurance Costs and More Red Flags in Lyft's IPO. Retrieved March 21, 2019 from https://finance.yahoo.com/news/swelling-insurance-costs-more-red-134329011.html

137. Jenkins, A. (2017, April 18). Why Uber Doesn't Want a Built-In Tipping Option. Retrieved January 25, 2019 from http://fortune.com/2017/04/18/uber-tipping-nyc/

138. Jenkins, I. H, Jahanshahi, M., Jueptner, M., Passingham, R. E., & Brooks, D. J. (2000). Self-initiated Versus Externally Triggered

Movements: II. The Effect of Movement Predictability on Regional Cerebral
23. Blood Flow. Brain, Volume 123, Issue 6, 1 June 2000, Pages 1216–1228,
https://doi.org/10.1093/brain/123.6.1216

139. Jingjing Jiang. More Americans Are Using Ride-Hailing Apps. Pew
Research Center, 4 Jan. 2019, www.pewresearch.org/fact-
tank/2019/01/04/more-americans-are-using-ride-hailing-apps/.

140. Keith Chen, Associate Professor Economics. UCLA Anderson School of
Management. https://www.anderson.ucla.edu/faculty_pages/keith.chen/

141. Keith Chen, M & E. Rossi, Peter & Oehlsen, Emily. (2017). The Value of
Flexible Work: Evidence from Uber Drivers. SSRN Electronic Journal.
10.2139/ssrn.2952556.

142. Kennedy, P. (January 2012). Why Dallas Leads the Nation in Drunk-
Driving Deaths. DMagazine. Retrieved January
17, 2019 from https://www.dmagazine.com/publications/d-
magazine/2012/january/why-dallas-leads-nation-in-drunkdriving-deaths/

143. Kircher, Malone. "How Uber Got Here." Intelligencer, 8 Mar. 2017,
nymag.com/intelligencer/article/dramatic-history-ride-hailing-app-uber-and-
ceo-kalanick.html.

144. Kleinman, Z. (2017, June 21). Uber: The scandals that drove Travis
Kalanick out. BBC. Retrieved January 18, 2019 from
https://www.bbc.com/news/technology-40352868

145. Kooti, F., Grbovic, M., Aiello, L. M., Djuric, N., Radosavljevic, V., &
Lerman, K. (2017). Analyzing Uber's Ridesharing Economy. 2017
International World Wide Web Conference Committee (IW3C2). WWW'17
Companion, April 3–7, 2017, Perth, Australia.
http://dx.doi.org/10.1145/3041021.3054194

146. Korosec, K. (2017, September 27). Uber Closes Xchange Leasing After
Losing $9,000 Per Car. Retrieved January 27, 2019 from
http://fortune.com/2017/09/27/uber-closes-xchange-leasing-after-losing-9000-
per-car/

147. Korosec, Kirsten. "Uber Freight Is Expanding into Europe –
TechCrunch." TechCrunch, 20 Mar. 2019,
techcrunch.com/2019/03/20/uber-freight-is-expanding-into-europe/.

148. Kovach, S. (2019, February 15). New York Taxi Workers Alliances.
Retrieved February 16, 2019 from https://www.cnbc.com/2019/02/15/uber-
sues-new-york-city-over-license-cap.html

149. Krisher, Tom. "5 Reasons Autonomous Cars Aren't Coming Anytime
Soon." SFGate, San Francisco Chronicle, 5
Feb. 2019, www.sfgate.com/business/article/5-reasons-autonomous-cars-aren-
t-coming-anytime-13588675.php.

150. Kristhof, K. (2017, July 24). How Amazon uses "surge pricing," just like
Uber. CBS News. Retrieved January 20,
2019 from https://www.cbsnews.com/news/amazon-surge-pricing-are-you-
getting-ripped-off-small-business/

151. Lawler, R. Uber Study Shows Its Drivers Make More Per Hour And
Work Fewer Hours Than Taxi Drivers. Quora.
Retrieved January 18, 2019 from https://techcrunch.com/2015/01/22/uber-
study/

152. Lebeau, Phil (Lebeaucarnews). "Waymo Starts Commercial Ride-Share Service ." CNBC, 5 Dec. 2018, https://www.cnbc.com/2018/12/05/waymo-starts-commercial-ride-share-service.html

153. LeCun, Y., Bengio, Y., & Hinton, G. (2015). Deep Learning. Nature volume 521, pages 436–444.

154. Libet, B., Gleason, C. A., Wright, E. W., & Pearl, D. K. (1983). Time of Conscious Intention to Act in Relation to Onset of Cerebral Activity (Readiness-Potential) the Unconscious Initiation of a Freely Voluntary Act. Brain (1983), 106, 623-642

155. Luo, M. (2004, July 7). Study of Taxi Drivers Finds More Immigrants at Wheel. Retrieved January 16, 2019 from https://www.nytimes.com/2004/07/07/nyregion/study-of-taxi-drivers-nds-more-immigrants-at-wheel.html

156. Lyft Blog. One Billion Rides. One Billion Connections. (2018, September 18) Retrieved March 21, 2019 from https://blog.lyft.com/posts/one-billion-rides

157. Lyft Funding Rounds. Retrieved January 18, 2019 from https://www.crunchbase.com/organization/lyft#section- funding-rounds

158. Lyft. Inclusion & Diversity. Retrieved March 21, 2019 from https://take.lyft.com/diversity/

159. Lyft. Meet the Lyft Driver Advisory Council. Retrieved January 26, 2019 from https://thehub.lyft.com/dac/

160. Lynn, M., McCall, M. (2000). Gratitude and Gratuity: A Meta-Analysis of Research on the Service-Tipping Relationship. Journal of Socio-Economics 29 (2000) 203-214

161. Maciag, Mike. (2014, February 25). "Public Transportation's Demographic Divide." Governing, www.governing.com/topics/transportation-infrastructure/gov-public-transportation-riders-demographic-divide-for-cities.html#data.

162. Marotti, A. (2018, October 22). Uber is testing an on-demand stang business in Chicago. Retrieved January 26, 2019 from https://www.chicagotribune.com/business/ct-biz-uber-works-chicago-20181019-story.html

163. Marshall, A. (2019, January 8). A Third of Americans Use Ride-Hail. Uber and Lyft Need More. Retrieved January 24, 2019 from https://www.wired.com/story/uber-lyft-ride-hail-stats-pew-research/

164. Maugh II, T. H. (2007, August 27). Benjamin Libet, 91; physiologist probed consciousness. Retrieved January 24, 2019 from http://articles.latimes.com/2007/aug/27/local/me-libet27

165. Maxwell, T. (2019, March 19). Lyft and Uber's plans to go public, explained. Retrieved May 15, 2019 from https://www.pbs.org/newshour/economy/making-sense/lyft-and-ubers-plans-to-go-public-explained

166. McGee, Chantel. "Only 4% of Uber Drivers Remain on the Platform a Year Later, Says Report." CNBC, 20 Apr. 2017, www.cnbc.com/2017/04/20/only-4-percent-of-uber-drivers-remain-after-a-year-says-report.html.

167. Mckinsey Global Institute. (2016, October). "Independent Work: Choice, Necessity, And The Gig Economy." Mckinsey& Company. Retrieved April 21, 2019 from
https://www.mckinsey.com/~/media/McKinsey/Featured%20Insights/Employment%20and%20Growth/Independent%20work%20Choice%20necessity%20and%20the%20gig%20economy/Independent-Work-Choice-necessity-and-the-gig-economy-Executive-Summary.ashx

168. Meng, Fanxing & Li, Shuling & Cao, Lingzhi & Li, Musen & Peng, Qijia & Wang, Chunhui & Zhang, Wei. (2014). Driving Fatigue in Professional Drivers: A Survey of Truck and Taxi Drivers. Traffic Injury Prevention. 16.10.1080/15389588.2014.973945.

169. Mercer, C & Macaulay, T. (2019, Mar 12). Which companies are making driverless cars? Techworld. Retrieved April 21, 2019 from
https://www.techworld.com/picture-gallery/data/-companies-working-on-driverless-cars-3641537/

170. Mercer, Christina, and Tom Macaulay. "Companies Working On Driverless Cars You Should Know About." Techworld, 12 Mar. 2019, www.techworld.com/picture-gallery/data/-companies-working-on-driverless-cars-3641537/.

171. Merriam-Webster Dictionary. Retrieved February 21, 2019 from https://www.merriam- webster.com/dictionary/%C3%BCber-

172. Mishel, L. (2018, May 15). Uber and the labor market. Uber drivers' compensation, wages, and the scale of Uber and the gig economy. Retrieved January 24, 2019 from https://www.epi.org/publication/uber-and-the-labor-market-uberdrivers-compensation-wages-and-the-scale-of-uber-and-the-gig-economy/

173. Mobile Fact Sheet. (2018, February 5). Retrieved January 18, 2019 from http://www.pewinternet.org/fact-sheet/mobile/

174. Molla, Rani. "Lyft Has Eaten into Uber's U.S. Market Share, New Data Suggests." Vox, 12 Dec. 2018, www.recode.net/2018/12/12/18134882/lyft-uber-ride-car-market-share.

175. Morris, A. G. (1993). "Changing Demographics of the Taxi Workforce: Implications for Taxi Driver Education." Presented at the 72nd Annual Meeting of the Transportation Research Board. Retrieved January 16, 2019 from
http://www.utrc2.org/sites/default/files/pubs/Changing-Demographics-of-Taxi-Workforce.pdf

176. Morris, D. Z. (2018, July 21). Uber Drivers Are Employees, New York Unemployment Insurance Board Rules. Fortune. Retrieved January 20, 2019 from http://fortune.com/2018/07/21/uber-drivers-employees-new-york-unemployment/

177. National Research Council of the National Academies (2005). History and Status of the U.S. Road System. In "Assessing and Managing the Ecological Impacts of Paved Roads (pp. 37-61)." Washington, D.C. The National Academies Press. Retrieved January 17, 2019 from https://www.nap.edu/read/11535/chapter/4

178. Nelson, Leah. "Understanding Transportation as a Service's Potential to Reduce Car Ownership." Mobility Lab, 7 Dec. 2018,

mobilitylab.org/2018/12/06/understanding-transportation-as-a-services-potential-to-reduce-car-ownership/.

179. Newcomer, E. (2017, February 28). In Video, Uber CEO Argues With Driver Over Falling Fares. Retrieved February 12, 2019 from https://www.bloomberg.com/news/articles/2017-02-28/in-video-uber-ceo-argues-with-driver-overfalling-fares

180. Newcomer, E. (2019, February 15). Uber Revenue Growth Slows, Losses Persist as 2019 IPO Draws Near. Retrieved March 21, 2019 from https://www.bloomberg.com/news/articles/2019-02-15/uber-results-show-revenue-growthslows-amid-persistent-losses

181. NHTSA Traffic Safety Fact 2017 Data. "Alcohol-Impaired Driving." Dept. of Transportation. https://crashstats.nhtsa.dot.gov/Api/Public/ViewPublication/812630

182. Nield, D. (2017, July 23). All the Sensors in Your Smartphone, and How They Work. Retrieved January 20, 2019 from https://gizmodo.com/all-the-sensors-in-your-smartphone-and-how-they-work-1797121002

183. NTTA System Map - NTTA GIS Home. Retrieved February 3, 2019 from https://maps.ntta.org/documents/MapGallery/NTTA%20System%20Map_20180530.pdf

184. O'Donnell, P. This Dallas startup just hauled in $14.5 million to disrupt Uber, Lyft. Dallasnews. Retrieved May 15, 2019 from https://www.dallasnews.com/business/entrepreneurs/2019/01/22/dallas-startup-just-hauled-145-milliondisrupt-uber-lyft

185. O'Brien, S. A., Black, N., Devine, C., & Grin, D. (2018, April 30). CNN investigation: 103 Uber drivers accused of sexual assault or abuse. CNN. Retrieved January 22, 2019 from https://money.cnn.com/2018/04/30/technology/uber-driver-sexual-assault/index.html

186. Olson, Edwin, and Edwin Olson. "The Moore's Law for Self-Driving Vehicles." Medium, May Mobility, 27 Feb. 2019, medium.com/may-mobility/the-moores-law-for-self-driving-vehicles-b78b8861e184.

187. Pager, T., Palmer, E. (218, October 7). Uber Driver's Death Marks Seventh For-Hire Driver Suicide Within a Year. Retrieved February 12, 2019 from https://www.nytimes.com/2018/10/07/nyregion/uber-driver-suicide-for-hire-taxisnew-york.html

188. Pash A. (2010). Google Instant Filters Your Google Search Results As You Type. Retrieved January 18, 2019 from https://lifehacker.com/5632939/google-instant-filters-your-google-search-results-as-you-type

189. Perez, S. Lyft is launching a rider loyalty program in December. Retrieved January 27, 2019 from https://techcrunch.com/2018/11/12/lyft-is-launching-a-rider-loyalty-program-in-december/

190. Perfecting the Pickup. Retrieved January 18, 2019 from http://simonpan.com/work/uber/

191. Portland Bureau of Transportation, PBOT. (2017, April). Greyball Audit Report. https://cdn.londonreconnections.com/2013/GreyballAudit.pdf

192. Public Transportation and the Rise of the Transportation Network Industry. Transportation Workers Union of America. April 2017. Retrieved February 18, 2019, from https://www.twu.org/wp-content/uploads/2017/05/The-Emerging-Transportation-Network-Industry-040817.pdf

193. Razak v. Uber Techs., Inc. Civil Action NO. 16-573 (E.D. Pa. Dec. 14, 2016). Legal Research Tools from Casetext, casetext.com/case/razak-v-uber-techs-inc-2.

194. Reported List of Incidents Involving Uber and Lyft. Retrieved May 24, 2019 from https://www.atchisontransport.com/blog/reported-list-of-incidents-involving-uber-and-lyft/

195. Reuters . (2017, August 23). Investors Are Questioning the True Value of an Uber Ride. Retrieved January 19, 2019 from http://fortune.com/2017/08/23/uber-valuation-ride-pricing-investors/

196. Salinas, Sara (Saracsalinas). "Lyft Pops in Trading Debut, Settles to Modest Gains." CNBC, 29 Mar. 2019, www.cnbc.com/2019/03/29/lyft-ipo-stock-starts-trading-on-public-market.html.

197. Samuels, A. (May 29, 2017). Uber, Lyft return to Austin as Texas Gov. Abbott signs ride-hailing measure into law. Retrieved January 17, 2019 from https://www.texastribune.org/2017/05/29/texas-gov-greg-abbott-signs-measurecreating-statewide-regulations-rid/

198. Scarpinelli, L. (2017, October 4). Uber changes board structure in a bid to strengthen its governance. World Finance. Retrieved April 21, 2019 from https://www.worldfinance.com/strategy/uber-changes-board-structure-in-a-bid-tostrengthen-its-governance

199. Schaller Consulting. The New Automobility: Lyft, Uber and the Future of American Cities. 2018, July 25. http://www.schallerconsult.com/rideservices/automobility.pdf

200. Schaller Consulting. Unsustainable. 2017, February 27. http://schallerconsult.com/rideservices/unsustainable.pdf

201. SCOCAL, Dynamex Operations West, Inc. v. Superior Court , S222732 available at: (https://scocal.stanford.edu/opinion/dynamex-operations-west-inc-v-superior-court-34584) (last visited Friday May 24, 2019).

202. Search, V. (2019, February 11). Pedestrian Hit by Uber Driver Gets $1M Pre-Suit Settlement. Retrieved February 12, 2019 from https://www.law.com/dailybusinessreview/2019/02/11/pedestrian-hit-by-uber-driver-gets-1m-pre-suitsettlement/?slreturn=20190112020315

203. Selecting A BISAC Code - Book Industry Study Group, bisg.org/page/BISACSelection.

204. Sheivachman, A. (2018, September 28). Uber's Quest to Hit on Another Moonshot Product. Skift. Retrieved January 16, 2019, from https://skift.com/2018/09/28/ubers-quest-to-hit-on-another-moonshot-product/

205. Shipp, B. (2017, October 10). Contractor says Uber drove him to homelessness. Retrieved January 27, 2019 from

https://www.wfaa.com/article/news/contractor-says-uber-drove-him-to-homelessness/481997058

206. Siddiqui, F. (2019, March 26). Uber and Lyft slashed wages. Now California drivers are protesting their IPOs. Retrieved March 21, 2019 from https://www.washingtonpost.com/technology/2019/03/26/uber-lyft-slashed-wagesnow-california-drivers-are-protesting-their-ipos/?noredirect=on&utm_term=.55d86cc26f0d

207. Siekierska, Alicja. "Innisfil, Ontario Sticks with Its Uber-as-Public-Transit Plan, Extending Its Pilot Project." Financial Post, 15 Mar. 2018, business.financialpost.com/transportation/innisl-ontario-sticks-with-its-uber-as-publictransit-plan-extending-its-pilot-project.

208. Siemaszko, C. (2018, June 8). In the shadow of Uber's rise, taxi driver suicides leave cabbies shaken. NBC News. Retrieved January 23, 2019 from https://www.nbcnews.com/news/us-news/shadow-uber-s-rise-taxi-driver-suicidesleave-cabbies-shaken-n879281

209. Smith, Craig. "110 Amazing Uber Statistics, Demographics and Facts." DMR, 15 May 2019, expandedramblings.com/index.php/uber-statistics/.

210. Smith, Craig. "50 Interesting Lyft Statistics." DMR, 13 May 2019, expandedramblings.com/index.php/lyft-statistics/.

211. Taxi drivers & chauffeurs. Retrieved January 17, 2019 from https://datausa.io/profile/soc/533041/

212. Taylor, Timothy. "Richard Thaler: The 2017 Nobel Prize in Economics." conversableeconomist.blogspot.com/2017/10/richard-thaler-2017-nobel-prizein.html.

213. Texas Department of Transportation. (2018, April 20). "Crash Contributing Factors" 2017 Calendar Year 2017. Retrieved January 17, 2019 from http://ftp.dot.state.tx.us/pub/txdot-info/trf/crash_statistics/2017/21.pdf

214. Texas Department of Transportation. (2018, April 20). "Crashes and Injuries by County" Calendar Year 2017. Retrieved January 17, 2019 from http://ftp.dot.state.tx.us/pub/txdot-info/trf/crash_statistics/2017/13.pdf

215. Texas Department of Transportation. (2018, April 20). "Distracted Driver Crashes and Injuries by County" Calendar Year 2017. Retrieved January 17, 2019 from https://ftp.dot.state.tx.us/pub/txdot-info/trf/crash_statistics/2017/32.pdf

216. Texas Department of Transportation. (2018, April 20). "DUI (Alcohol) Involved Crashes by County" Calendar Year 2017. Retrieved January 17, 2019 from http://ftp.dot.state.tx.us/pub/txdot-info/trf/crash_statistics/2017/39.pdf

217. Texas Department of Transportation. (2018, April 20). "DUI (Alcohol) Related Total Crashes by Hour of the Day" Calendar Year 2017. Retrieved January 17, 2019 from http://ftp.dot.state.tx.us/pub/txdot-info/trf/crash_statistics/2017/48.pdf

218. Texas Department of Transportation. (2018, April 20). "DUI (Alcohol) Related Crashes by Hour and Day of the Week" Calendar Year 2017. http://ftp.dot.state.tx.us/pub/txdot-info/trf/crash_statistics/2017/45.pdf

219. Texas Department of Transportation. (2018, April 20). "Fatal Crashes and Fatalities by Month and Road Type" Calendar Year 2017. Retrieved January 17, 2019 from http://ftp.dot.state.tx.us/pub/txdot-info/trf/crash_statistics/2017/05.pdf

220. Texas Department of Transportation. (2018, April 20). "Fatalities by Age, Person Type, and Gender" Calendar Year 2017 (Excludes Motorcycles). Retrieved January 17, 2019 from http://ftp.dot.state.tx.us/pub/txdotinfo/trf/crash_statistics/2017/06.pdf

221. Texas Department of Transportation. (2018, April 20). "First Harmful Event of Crashes and Injuries by Severity" Calendar Year 2017. Retrieved January 17, 2019 from http://ftp.dot.state.tx.us/pub/txdot-info/trf/crash_statistics/2017/19.pdf

222. Texas Department of Transportation. (2018, April 20). "Speed Involved Crashes and Injuries by County" Calendar Year 2017. Retrieved January 17, 2019 from http://ftp.dot.state.tx.us/pub/txdot-info/trf/crash_statistics/2017/22.pdf

223. Texas Department of Transportation. (2018, April 20). "Statewide Traffic Crash Rates" Calendar Year 2017. Retrieved January 17, 2019 from http://ftp.dot.state.tx.us/pub/txdot-info/trf/crash_statistics/2017/02.pdf

224. Texas Department of Transportation. (2018, April 20). "Texas Motor Vehicle Crash Statistics" - 2017. https://www.txdot.gov/government/enforcement/annual-summary.html

225. Texas Department of Transportation. (2018, April 20). "Texas Motor Vehicle Traffic Crash Facts" Calendar Year 2017. Retrieved January 17, 2019 from http://ftp.dot.state.tx.us/pub/txdot-info/trf/crash_statistics/2017/01.pdf

226. Texas Department of Transportation. (2018, April 20). "Weather Conditions for Crashes" Calendar Year 2017. Retrieved January 17, 2019 from http://ftp.dot.state.tx.us/pub/txdot-info/trf/crash_statistics/2017/24.pdf

227. Texas Department of Transportation. "Crashes and Injuries Cities and Towns" Calendar Year 2017. Retrieved January 17, 2019 from http://ftp.dot.state.tx.us/pub/txdot-info/trf/crash_statistics/2017/14.pdf

228. Texas Dept. of Transportation. "DUI (Alcohol) Crashes and Injuries by County." 2017. http://ftp.dot.state.tx.us/pub/txdot-info/trf/crash_statistics/2017/40.pdf

229. Texas Transportation by the Numbers: Meeting the State's Need for Safe and Efficient Mobility. (2014). TRIP. Retrieved January 17, 2019 from http://www.tripnet.org/docs/TX_Transportation_by_the_Numbers_TRIP_Report_July_2014.pdf

230. The New York City Taxi and Limousine Commission (TLC). 2018 TLC Factbook. Retrieved January 27, 2019 from www.nyc.gov/html/tlc/downloads/pdf/2018_tlc_factbook.pdf

231. The New York City Taxi and Limousine Commission. 2014 Taxicab Factbook. Retrieved March 21, 2019 from https://www1.nyc.gov/assets/tlc/downloads/pdf/2014_tlc_factbook.pdf

232. The World Bank. Belt and Road Initiative. (2018, March 29). Retrieved April 21, 2019 from

https://www.worldbank.org/en/topic/regional-integration/brief/belt-and-road-initiative

233. Thompson, D. (2018, November 12). Amazon's HQ2 Spectacle Isn't Just Shameful—It Should Be Illegal. The Atlantic. Retrieved January 18, 2019 from https://www.theatlantic.com/ideas/archive/2018/11/amazons-hq2-spectacleshould-be-illegal/575539/

234. Todd Litman (2019, March 18). Autonomous Vehicle Implementation Predictions, Implications for Transport Planning. Victoria Transport Policy Institute. Retrieved April 21, 2019 from https://www.vtpi.org/avip.pdf

235. TollRoad Marketing. North Texas Tollway Authority, NTTA. Retrieved February 1, 2019 from https://tollperks.com

236. Toor, A. (2015, October 20). Uber driver found guilty of raping female passenger in India. The Verge. Retrieved April 21, 2019 from https://www.theverge.com/2015/10/20/9573003/uber-india-rape-delhi-guilty-verdict

237. Topic: Uber Technologies- Statistics & Facts. Retrieved January 16, 2019, from https://www.statista.com/topics/4826/uber-technologies/

238. Transportation Cost and Benefit Analysis II–Roadway Costs. Victoria Transport Policy Institute. 2018, April 24. http://www.vtpi.org/tca/tca0506.pdf

239. Transportation Cost and Benet Analysis Techniques, Estimates and Implications. Victoria Transport Policy Institute. Second Edition. 2009, January 2. http://www.vtpi.org/tca/tca01.pdf

240. Uber Blog. Driver Announcements. Rates to better value your time. Retrieved February 9, 2019 from https://www.ubercom/blog/phoenix/rates-to-better-value-your-time/?state=d4iYuINLBqh8sXYhTdPHP6i4Nj91g6cobFbr_odfLok%3D&_csid=_7Up13w2moyDiv4tYmkX1w#_

241. Uber driver accused of sexually assaulting rider is taken into ICE custody. Retrieved February 12, 2019 from https://www.wcvb.com/article/uber-driver-accused-of-sexually-assaulting-rider-taken-into-ice-custody-faces-felonycharge/26282974

242. Uber Funding Rounds. Retrieved January 18, 2019 from https://www.crunchbase.com/organization/uber/funding_rounds/funding_rounds_list#section-funding-rounds

243. Uber Help. How are Long Pickup Premiums calculated? Retrieved February 9, 2019 from https://help.uber.com/partners/article/how-are-long-pickup-premiums-calculated?nodeId=20d33df7-7317-4f86-aa38-5db09a219c27#_

244. Uber Help. Request a ride with multiple stops. Retrieved February 2, 2019 from https://help.uber.com/riders/article/request-a-ride-with-multiple-stops?nodeId=26f09874-91e9-4fe1-9537-ec680a47ecbe

245. Uber Newsroom. (2015, December 7). New Survey: Drivers Choose Uber for its Flexibility and Convenience. Retrieved April 21, 2019 from https://www.uber.com/newsroom/driver-partner-survey/

246. Uber Newsroom. (2017, August 30). Uber's New CEO. Retrieved April 21, 2019 from https://www.uber.com/newsroom/ubers-new-ceo-3

247. Uber Newsroom. (2018, July 28). Uber in the Economy. Retrieved April 21, 2019 from https://www.uber.com/newsroom/uber-in-the-economy/

248. Uber Newsroom. (2019, March 1). Insurance for Ridesharing Drivers with Uber in New York. Retrieved April 21, 2019 from https://www.uber.com/newsroom/nys-ridesharing-insurance/

249. Uber Newsroom. (2019, March 20). Uber Freight launches in Europe. Retrieved April 21, 2019 from https://www.uber.com/newsroom/uber-freight-launches-in-europe/

250. Uber Newsroom. History. Retrieved March 21, 2019 from https://www.uber.com/newsroom/history/

251. Uber. Can I bring someone with me while I'm online? Retrieved January 17, 2019 from https://help.uber.com/partners/article/can-i-bring-someone-with-me-while-im-online-?nodeId=9db0159e-437e-4932-bbd2-59002f83adde

252. Uber. Company Info. Retrieved March 21, 2019 from https://www.uber.com/newsroom/company-info/

253. Uber. Diversity and Inclusion. Retrieved March 21, 2019 from https://www.uber.com/about/diversity/

254. Uber. Insurance. Retrieved January 27, 2019 from https://help.uber.com/partners/article/insurance-?nodeId=a4afb2ed-75af-4db6-8fdb-dccecfcc3fd7

255. Uber. Partner Injury Protection. Accident insurance from Old Mutual Insurance. Retrieved April 21, 2019 from https://www.uber.com/drive/insurance/

256. Uber. Payments and Earnings. Retrieved April 21, 2019 from https://www.uber.com/en-GH/drive/resources/payments/?state=DB56dPvme9UY9A8ZL7BcfjYbCiG7Z TeqV8RDyXPK4eo%3D&_csid=woobt28HbR3bWJGsXfCa0Q#_

257. Uber. What is dynamic pricing? Retrieved January 18, 2019 from https://help.uber.com/riders/article/what-is-dynamic-pricing-?nodeId=34212e8b-d69a-4d8a-a923-095d3075b487

258. United Nations. "68% of the world population projected to live in urban areas by 2050, says UN."
Retrieved May 15, 2019 from https://www.un.org/development/desa/en/news/population/2018-revisionof-world-urbanization- prospects.html

259. United States Securities and Exchange Commission. Amendment No. 2 to Form S-1 Registration
Statement Under The Securities Act Of 1933 Lyft, Inc. Retrieved March 21, 2019 from
https://www.sec.gov/Archives/edgar/data/1759509/000119312519088569/d72 1841ds1a.htm

260. United States Securities and Exchange Commission. Lyft Form S-1 Registration Statement. Retrieved May 15, 2019 from https://www.sec.gov/Archives/edgar/data/1759509/000119312519059849/ d633517ds1.htm

261. United States Securities and Exchange Commission. Uber Form S-1 Registration Statement. Retrieved May 15, 2019 from https://www.sec.gov/Archives/edgar/data/1543151/000119312519103850/d647752ds1.htm

262. United States Securities and Exchange Commission. Update to Uber Form S-1 Registration Statement. Retrieved May 15, 2019 from https://www.sec.gov/Archives/edgar/data/1543151/000119312519142095/d727902dfwp.htm

263. US Department of Transportation. NHTSA, 13 May 2019. Speeding. www.nhtsa.gov/risky-driving/speeding

264. US Dept. of Labor. Bureau of Labor Statistics. Occupational Employment and Wages, May 2017. 53-3041 Taxi Drivers and Chauffeurs. Retrieved April 21, 2019 from https://www.bls.gov/oes/2017/may/oes533041.htm

265. US Dept. of Transportation. NHTSA. Traffic Safety Facts 2016

266. Valle, G. D. (2019, February 1). Uber prices in NYC are about to go up, because drivers are getting a wage hike. Vox. https://www.vox.com/the-goods/2019/2/1/18207332/uber-nyc-price-increase-wage-law

267. Vartabedian, Ralph. "Bullet-Train Land Acquisitions Are Moving so Slowly a Judge Hearing the Cases Calls It a 'Lifetime Job'." Los Angeles Times, Los Angeles Times, 20 Nov. 2018, www.latimes.com/local/california/la-me-bullet- judge-201801120-story.html.

268. Vedantam, S. (Host). (2016, May 17). This Is Your Brain On Uber [Audio podcast]. NPR. Retrieved January 20, 2019 from https://www.npr.org/2016/05/17/478266839/this-is-your-brain-on-uber

269. Vedantam, S. (Host). (2017, October 23). Misbehaving with Richard Thaler. [Audio podcast]. NPR. Retrieved January 23, 2019 from https://www.npr.org/templates/transcript/transcript.php?storyId=559511691

270. Vedantam, S. (Host). (2017, October 23). Predictably Unpredictable: Why We Don't Act Like We Should. [Audio podcast]. NPR. Retrieved February 3, 2019 from https://www.npr.org/2017/10/23/559581601/predictably-unpredictable-why-we-dont-act-like-we-should

271. Venkatesan, M. (2018, May 7). Artificial Intelligence vs. Machine Learning vs. Deep Learning. https://www.datasciencecentral.com/profiles/blogs/artificial-intelligence-vs-machine-learning-vs-deep- learning

272. Virginia Dept. of Transportation, VDOT. I-81 Corridor Improvement Study http://www.virginiadot.org/projects/resources/5-LOS_descriptions.pdf

273. Wakabayashi, D. (2018, March 19). Self-Driving Uber Car Kills Pedestrian in Arizona, Where Robots Roam. New York Times. Retrieved January 18, 2019 from https://www.nytimes.com/2018/03/19/technology/uber-driverless- fatality.html

274. Welch, C. (2016, January 6). Uber will pay $20,000 Fine in settlement over 'God View' tracking. The Verge. Retrieved April 21, 2019 from

https://www.theverge.com/2016/1/6/10726004/uber-god-modesettlement-fine

275. WGN Web Desk and Lewis, S. (2019, February 11). Passengers ask Uber driver to stop for cigarettes and then steal his car. Retrieved February 12, 2019 from https://wgntv.com/2019/02/11/passengersask-uber-driver-to-stop-for-cigarettes- and-then-steal-his-car/

276. Who Are Uber's Biggest Competitors? (2017, October 17). Retrieved January 27, 2019 from https://www.nasdaq.com/article/who-are-ubers-biggest-competitors-cm860923

277. Wiessner, D. (2018, April 12). U.S. judge says Uber drivers are not company's employees. Reuters. Retrieved January 20, 2019 from https://www.reuters.com/article/us-uber-lawsuit/u-s-judge-says-uberdrivers-are-not-companys- employees-idUSKBN1HJ31I

278. Wiggers, Kyle. "5 Companies Are Testing 55 Self-Driving Cars in Pittsburgh." VentureBeat, 26 Apr. 2019, venturebeat.com/2019/04/26/5-companies-are-testing-55-self-driving-cars-in-pittsburgh/.

279. Wong, J. C, and Morris, S. Collision course: Uber's terrible 2017. The Guardian. Retrieved April 21, 2019 from https://www.theguardian.com/technology/ng-interactive/2017/dec/27/uber-2017-scandalsinvestigation

280. Zetlin, M. (2016, October 29). Uber Drivers Are Employees Not Contractors, British Court Rules. Retrieved January 20, 2019 from https://www.inc.com/minda-zetlin/uber-drivers-are-employees-notcontractors-british-court-rules.html

INDEX

Index

Index

Index

X

Y

Z

www.ingramcontent.com/pod-product-compliance
Lightning Source LLC
Chambersburg PA
CBHW071242050326
40690CB00011B/2229